D1157721

ıted him with the

VIRGIN LANDS
Two Years in Kazakhstan, 1954-5

by

L. I. BREZHNEV

PERGAMON PRESS

OXFORD · NEW YORK · TORONTO · SYDNEY · PARIS · FRANKFURT

U.K.	Pergamon Press Ltd., Headington Hill Hall, Oxford OX3 0BW, England
U.S.A.	Pergamon Press Inc., Maxwell House, Fairview Park, Elmsford, New York 10523, U.S.A.
CANADA	Pergamon of Canada, Suite 104, 150 Consumers Road, Willowdale, Ontario M2J 1P9, Canada
AUSTRALIA	Pergamon Press (Aust.) Pty. Ltd., P.O. Box 544, Potts Point, N.S.W. 2011, Australia
FRANCE	Pergamon Press SARL, 24 rue des Ecoles, 75240 Paris, Cedex 05, France
FEDERAL REPUBLIC OF GERMANY	Pergamon Press GmbH, 6242 Kronberg-Taunus, Pferdstrasse 1, Federal Republic of Germany

First edition 1979

British Library Cataloguing in Publication Data

Brezhnev, Leonid Il'ich.
Virgin Lands
1. Brezhnev, Leonid Il'ich 2. Statesmen - Russia - Biography.
I. Title
947.085'0924   DK275.B7   79-42773
ISBN 0-08-023584-0
ISBN 0-08-023583-2 Pbk

Printed and bound in Great Britain by
William Clowes (Beccles) Limited, Beccles and London

CONTENTS

LIST OF ILLUSTRATIONS

Map: The Virgin Lands of Kazakhstan, p. 11

(between pp. 8/9)

Brezhnev as First Secretary in Kazakhstan
Tractor-driven ploughing
With experts at a state farm
At a conference in Kazakhstan, 1954

(between pp. 40/41)

Among virgin landers, winter
Early settlers: the barber's shop
   Cooking breakfast
   Erecting a tent
   YCL members leave Leningrad
L. M. Kartauzov
I. I. Ivanov

(between pp. 62/63)

A state farm
Newly-built grain elevator
Loading grain
Award to Urneksky State Grain Farm, 1955
A "first furrow"
Kustanai: cereal production-complex, 1978
School at Lomonosov State Farm, 1978

(between pp. 84/85)

Young settlers today
Galya Gulyaeva, tractor driver
S. V. Kalchenko and agriculturalists
Award to Lomonosov State Farm, 1978
Reception for Brezhnev, Alma-Ata

1.

Let there be grain and the songs will come of themselves, people say. And with good reason. Grain has always been the staple product, the very basis of life. Even in our age of great scientific and technological advance it has remained the bedrock of the life of nations. People have broken through into outer space, they tame rivers, seas, oceans, they extract oil and gas from the bowels of the earth, they have mastered the energy of the atom, but grain is still grain.

The citizens of a land which has ears of grain in its coat of arms have an especially sensitive and sacred attitude towards grain. It is a feeling that I, too, have known since childhood.

My father was a worker, my grandfather a peasant, and I had a go at both factory and farm work. I began as a worker, but in the years of economic disruption, during long stoppages at the factory, I learned to plough, sow and reap and came to understand what it means to grow grain with one's own hands. I became a land-use surveyor, working in the villages of the Kursk Region, in Byelorussia and in the Urals, and even later, when I went back to metallurgy again, the exigencies of the time never allowed me to forget the importance of grain. Together with other Party members I went to the villages, argued it out with the kulaks at village meetings, and helped to organise the first collective farms.

I suppose you could say that it was only four years, not a long time, that I spent in the countryside. But looking at it another way, four years is a long time for a young man at the beginning of his working life. I began as a land-use surveyor at the very start of collectivisation and returned to the factory when the process had been essentially completed. Those years, from 1927 to 1931, amounted to a whole era in the life of the country. When we were allotting land to the agricultural co-operatives, we realised that we were not simply breaking down the old land boundaries, but helping in the socialist reorganisation of the countryside and the reordering of the whole ancient structure of peasant life.

I say this because I feel strong ties with both town and country, factory and field, industry and agriculture. In Zaporozhe, as I have already written, my main concern was the restoration of industry, but collective farm matters demanded constant attention as well. In Dnepropetrovsk my time was divided about equally between town and country. In Moldavia agriculture took first place, but industry, which in that area had to be virtually started from scratch, could not be left unattended. So my concerns ran side by side, like parallel lines, which are supposed never to intersect, but which in my case did.

And today, too, on my desk in the Kremlin I regularly find reports on the spring sowing, the condition of the young crops, and the rate of harvesting. I have an old habit of calling up various zones of the country, and when I hear our comrades speaking from the Kuban, the Dnieper, Moldavia, the Volga or Siberia, I can tell by their voices how their crops are going. In the virgin lands, for instance, if there has been no rain before 15 June, I know that several centners* will have to be deducted from the yield. If there is no rain right up till the end of the month, knock off some more . . . At such moments I look out of my window here in Moscow and see nothing but the endless expanse of the new lands, the worried faces of the combine operators, the agronomists, the Party district committee officials and, though far away from these good friends, I again feel as if I were at their side.

The development of the virgin lands is part of my life. It all began on a frosty Moscow day at the end of January 1954, when I was sum-

*centner 100 kilograms. Used in measuring grain yields per hectare.

moned to the Central Committee. The problem was familiar to me already and this was not the first time I had heard about the virgin lands; what was new was that I would be entrusted with their development on a massive scale. The project was to be launched in Kazakhstan in the coming spring and the schedule was tight. It would be a tough assignment and no one tried to hide the fact. But they also said that at that moment no task was more important, and that the Central Committee had decided to send P. K. Ponomarenko and me to tackle it.

The crucial factor, they told me, was that things in Kazakhstan were not in very good shape. The local leadership was locked into its old ways and would probably not be equal to the new tasks. To bring these virgin lands under the plough would require a different level of understanding of all that we would have to accomplish in these far-flung steppes.

Our main task was to open up the virgin lands. This, I knew, would present great difficulties. Above all, it was essential to find the right organisational solution for such an important task. It was not just a matter of boosting grain production in one republic but of providing a fundamental solution to the grain problem for the whole Soviet Union.

The virgin lands had to produce a grain harvest that very autumn! That autumn, without fail!

So once again, not for the first or last time, an abrupt change occurred in my life.

On 30 January, 1954, the Presidium of the Central Committee met to discuss the situation in Kazakhstan and the tasks connected with the virgin lands project. Two days later I left by plane for Alma-Ata.

It never occurred to me then that years later I should feel the urge to tell people about that unforgettable period in my life. As at other stages in my career, I kept no diary or notes. There were too many other things to do. But it's not something worth worrying about.

I recall the postscript that Lenin wrote to his book *The State and Revolution*. He had been going to write one more chapter but in fact never got around to it because the October Revolution intervened. "Such an 'interruption' ", he remarks with some humour, "can only be welcomed. It is more pleasant and useful to go through 'the experience of the revolution' than to write about it." Those words of Lenin's are a reminder to us all.

In the virgin lands, millions of Soviet people continued to go through the experience of the revolution and multiplied its achievements in new historical conditions. They had the vital experience of building developed socialism. So I shall always cherish the memory of those years devoted entirely to the virgin lands.

It was the first time I had ever been to Alma-Ata but I already had a warm affection for the city when I took my first look at it. It had won a place in my heart long ago. I had loved it from a distance, just as much as I loved Kamenskoe, Dnepropetrovsk or Zaporozhe.

Like many other people serving at the front, I had a long wait before receiving the address of the place to which my family had been evacuated. It had taken eight long and anxious months for the first letter from my wife with her return address on it (95 Karl Marx St, Alma-Ata) to reach me at the front. And it was from that letter that I learnt the names of the people who had given shelter to my family—the Baibusynovs, Tursun Tarabaevich and his wife Rukya Yarulovna. I eventually found their little house, so much like the thousands of others in the almost entirely one-storey Alma-Ata of those days. My wife had written to me during the war that in summer the house was buried in greenery and there had been a murmuring *aryk** under the window. But now it was February, the *aryk* had run dry and the bare branches of the trees were dripping as the thaw approached. For some reason I had a sudden vivid recall of my

---

*aryk irrigation ditch or canal.

wartime days. Should I go in? Surely I should say thank you to that kind Kazakh family and bow to the walls of a house where seven people instead of four had managed to live happily together during those stressful years. But I decided to wait until my wife arrived and then, if it was at all possible, go and see them together.

I continued my walk, knowing that this was the best way of forming a first impression of the city where I was to live and work. I took a look at the bazaar, which can reveal a lot to an experienced eye. It's a kind of barometer of the economic life of any locality, a mirror of the customs and traditions of its population. The Alma-Ata bazaar, noisy, crowded, kaleidoscopic, yielded a good deal of useful information and I felt intimately attracted by the whole colourful image that the city presented.

As things worked out, I lived at several different addresses there. The first was out of town, at a resort about five kilometres from the now famous Medeo skating rink (it had not been built in those days). It was an extremely beautiful place. Orchards, footpaths, pure air, a babbling stream running down from the mountains. And the mountains themselves were all round us with their deep-blue shadows and glistening snowy peaks. During my most recent visit to Kazakhstan, in September 1976, I called at the rest home I had stayed in and decided to find my old room. I went up confidently to the first floor, spotted a familiar-looking door and started telling the people with me that there used to be a desk by the window and a sofa beside it.

"No, Leonid Ilyich," the housekeeper told me, "you are a whole two doors out."

This incident testifies not so much to the imperfections of human memory as to the rapidity of change. It was not just the rest home that had been reconstructed; the whole of present-day Alma-Ata is quite different from the old town. Now it is a large modern city with a population close to a million, a beautiful place with a character all its own. It is being rebuilt on a sweeping scale, but according to a well-thought-out plan and, I would say, with a great deal of loving care. You don't see any depressing, monotonous districts. The architecture of the new areas is original and none of the major buildings repeat themselves.

Whenever I pay them one of my flying visits, I say to my old friends, "Here I am again, visiting you like my own kith and kin!" When my family moved to Alma-Ata, we made our home in a small wooden peasant-type house in the same old district as the rest home, in an area known as Little Ravine. Now the house has been pulled down. Later on we moved to an experimental house made of sandstone blocks in Dzhambul Street, in the centre of the city. Apparently those blocks were not very durable because the building is no longer standing. Nor is the little cottage that sheltered my family during the war. In its place there is a large fountain, playing merrily. Only one of the houses we lived in, on the corner of Furmanov and Kurmangazy Streets, has survived to this day. But I lived there only in the last few months of my time in Alma-Ata.

At the beginning of February 1954, almost before I had time to look round the new place, I had to attend a plenary meeting of the Kazakh Central Committee. Many of the speakers at the meeting spoke out strongly, and were critical of their own work. Ponomarenko and I listened attentively, but did not speak ourselves. When voting time came round, a representative of the CPSU Central Committee told the plenum that the Presidium of the Central Committee recommended that Ponomarenko should be elected first secretary and Brezhnev, second secretary.

Ponomarenko and I worked in close contact, both dedicated to the same goal, and sharing the same numerous anxieties and burdens. For my part I had always valued and respected Panteleimon Kondratevich, both as the "chief partisan", who all through the war had directed the popular resistance movement operating behind the enemy lines, and as a skilled organiser and reliable comrade.

At the end of the meeting he thanked the participants and said only a few words on behalf of the two of us:

"I hope we will be able to justify your trust. We will work and work hard! I think that within the next two years we will be able to report to the Central Committee that the tasks assigned to the Kazakhstan Party organisation have been fulfilled."

And so it was, exactly two years later, when I had become first secretary of the Kazakh Communist Party's Central Committee, that I reported to the 20th Party Congress that the Party's great task of bringing the virgin lands under cultivation had been fulfilled with distinction.

2.

We were all up to our ears in work from the start. Today, after so many years, looking through the documents of those days I sometimes wonder how we managed to get so much done, and all of it on time. But apparently the human organism is built to adapt to incredible strains, both nervous and physical. Again one recalls the war. The people who took part in it were stretched to the limits of human endurance. They went short of sleep and food, they got soaked in the trenches, they lay for days on end in the snow, they plunged into icy water, and yet hardly anyone suffered from colds and other "peacetime" ills. Something similar was to be seen in the virgin lands.

I have already compared the great epic of the virgin lands to a wartime front, to a great battle won by the Party and the people. The memory of the war will always be with us frontline men, and it is, after all, an accurate enough comparison. Of course, in the virgin lands there was no shooting, no bombing, no shelling, but all the rest was like a real battle.

To begin with, speaking in the same military terms, the first thing to do was to regroup our forces and bring up our reserves. This was no simple matter. After the plenum came the Seventh Congress of the Communist Party of Kazakhstan, at which the situation was analysed and the work of the previous Central Committee Buro and Secretariat was found to have been unsatisfactory.

I will explain why. In a land of very rich natural resources, with hundreds of collective farms, state farms and tractor stations, a land where the fields were worked by tens of thousands of tractors and combines, where besides the arable land there were millions of hectares of hayfields and pastures, the production of grain, meat, cotton and wool had not increased above the pre-war level, and in some instances had actually fallen below it. Milk yields were lower than in 1940, grain crops averaged only 5 or 6 centners per hectare, cotton only 10 centners, and potatoes not more than 60 centners.

By that time even such war-devastated areas as the Kuban, the Ukraine and the Don had recovered and begun to build up their harvests and the productivity of their animal breeding. But here, although the 1953 weather had been exceptionally kind to the republic, one-and-a-half million head of cattle were lost because of low feed stocks. During the fierce winters animals were kept in the open, without even the primitive shelter of the *koshara**. "It has always been so in our country," people would say. I should add that of the chairmen of the collective farms many had only an elementary education, and three hundred were no more than semi-literate.

Of course, there were also objective reasons for the poor state of agriculture in Kazakhstan. If reflected the neglect of this vital branch of the economy throughout the country. This was described frankly and straightforwardly by the Party at the September 1953 Central Committee plenum. However, even against this general background the situation in Kazakhstan looked depressing. A further difficulty was that some of the local leadership had resigned

koshara an open cow shed or sheep-fold.

Brezhnev as First Secretary of the Kazakhstan Party.

"The virgin lands had to produce a grain harvest that very autumn!"

Fieldwork with experts at a state farm.

As Second Secretary on the Presidium, at a meeting in
Kazakhstan, 1954.

themselves to the state of affairs and acted on the principle of "we may be lucky".

"The administration of such a big republic was too much for us," Kazakh Central Committee secretary I. I. Afonov, who had been directly in charge of agriculture, stated at the congress. "Instead of being in control of events, we have been dashing about aimlessly like bad firemen. We merely fight the 'fires' that keep breaking out now in one place, now in another. Our basic form of administration is not the written instruction but the fellow on the spot."

After such admissions one would not be surprised by the lack of initiative on the part of the regional Party committees. If anyone did try to put matters right, they did so in a rather "original" way. Aktyubinsk Region, for instance, launched a campaign for laying in a year-and-a-half's supply of fodder. This praiseworthy objective was approved and the commitment was announced in the newspapers. But any initiative, as everyone knows, should rely mainly on internal resources, on existing but unused capacity. This is the chief value of such initiatives. But the Aktyubinsk people took a different course. After their resounding promises they sent a letter to the Kazakh Council of Ministers: in view of this, that and the other, for us to be able to fulfil our commitments, you must provide us at once with three hundred additional tractors, six thousand tons of kerosene, so much motor oil and gear grease, and spare parts. In short, help us to be heroes if you don't want to disgrace yourselves along with us.

All my experience of administrative work — Party, Soviet, army or in production — has long since convinced me that the tendency to sponge, the desire to put one's own affairs in order at the expense of others reveals as clearly as a litmus test what this or that person is capable of. And since we were going to bring virgin land under cultivation, and nation-wide help had been promised, such sponging could assume dangerous proportions. So I resolved to take special note of this phenomenon.

I have often spoken of the need to look after personnel. I have in mind, of course, people who have shown that they know how to work. It is not a matter of being all-forgiving: the incompetent and dishonest must be replaced without flinching. Here I could see for myself that some of the leaders at various levels were often promoted on the basis of patronage and influence. This had to be stamped out at once, and Ponomarenko and myself took a tough stand. So that there should be no misunderstandings, we announced the fact openly and straightforwardly. In one of my first speeches (before the electorate in Alma-Ata in March 1954) I said:

"In view of the enormous tasks now confronting the Kazakh Party organisation the importance of the correct personnel policy has immeasurably increased. The Seventh Congress of the Kazakh Communist Party has revealed serious shortcomings and mistakes in personnel work, which show that some leaders have lost their sense of responsibility and have selected personnel not according to their abilities, but on the principle of personal attachment. We cannot tolerate this. The republic has plenty of mature, experienced people, well qualified for promotion to positions of leadership and capable of performing the tasks set by the Party."

So we went on selecting strong leaders and bringing up our reserves, while waiting impatiently for the Party's decision to start opening up the virgin lands. And at the very end of February 1954 came the historic February-March Central Committee plenum, which passed the decision "on further increasing the country's grain production and cultivation of virgin and abandoned lands".

The great battle in the Kazakh steppes began. It was spread over a huge geographical area. Northern Kazakhstan extends 1,300 kilometres from East to West and 900 kilometres from North to South. The total area of its present six regions (there used to be five) — Kustanai, Tselinograd (formerly Akmolinsk), North Kazakhstan, Kokchetav, Turgai and Pavlodar — exceeds 600,000 square kilometres, much more than the whole territory of, say, France. And over this huge area we had to plough up 250,000

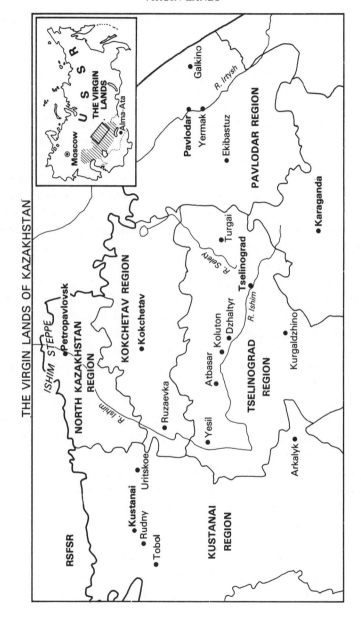

THE VIRGIN LANDS OF KAZAKHSTAN

square kilometres of fertile steppeland, an area larger than the whole of Britain.

Besides us, the Altai Territory, Krasnoyarsk Territory, Novosibirsk and Omsk Regions, the Volga country, the Urals and the Far East were also involved in the virgin lands project. As many people no doubt know, the area of virgin and abandoned lands brought under cultivation in the USSR now totals 42 million hectares, 25 million of which were ploughed in Kazakhstan. And 18 million of that total were opened up in the Kazakhstan steppes in 1954 and 1955.

These figures are striking, but the development of the virgin lands was not just a matter of ploughing. It meant housing, schools, hospitals, kindergartens, crèches, recreation centres and new roads, bridges, airfields and animal farms, grain elevators, storehouses, factories. In short, everything that people need to live a normal life and farm in a modern way.

I cannot give a detailed, day-by-day account of events. A good deal has already been written about the virgin lands project, the difficulties of its development, and about the lives and achievements of its pioneers. I will describe only the main directions of our work, the strategy and tactics that we adopted to make the virgin lands what they have become today: regulation of the use of land on the new farms and the old ones that had been expanded; selection of sites for the centres of the new state farms; the reception and accommodation of hundreds of thousands of volunteers in country that was still totally unprepared for human habitation; the urgent building of tens and, later, hundreds of state farm settlements; the selection of many thousands of specialists; the building of close-knit, harmonious collectives out of a heterogeneous mass of people; and the actual ploughing of the virgin soil and the first spring sowing. . . . And this had to be done not gradually but all at once, simultaneously.

To give the reader an idea, for example, of the scale of the work involved in strengthening the local leadership, work which had to be done in a very short time, I need only say that in 1954 alone we considered and recommended for work in the virgin lands more than five hundred new secretaries of district Party committees and secretaries of primary Party organisations, thousands of collective farm chairmen, agronomists, animal specialists, engineers and mechanics. They included a good many splendid local functionaries, and even more newcomers. The CPSU Central Committee, the central ministries, and many republics and regions who generously shared their personnel with the virgin lands were a tremendous help to us.

The central Ministry of State Farms set up a special headquarters for selecting personnel. Its offices reminded one of a railway station, there were so many people coming and going. I went there for weeks on end and sat from early morning till midnight interviewing candidates. I never grudged the time needed for a detailed and thorough talk with anyone who intended to go out to the virgin lands. It was important that everybody should realise the complexity and depth of the plan, acquire real faith in it and work to achieve it to the very best of his strength and ability. In the course of these conversations I would try to find out whether the person had a real desire to go, what experience he had, how healthy he was, and whether his family was prepared to move out there as well. The questions I was asked in return were no less numerous: when to go, how much land had this or that state farm, what kind of soil, where would the other people be from, how much machinery and equipment was being assigned there, what to take, and so on.

In the corridors of the ministry, between interviews, the future farm directors would recruit their specialists on the spot. This was how the famous quintets were formed: director, chief agronomist, chief engineer, construction engineer and chief accountant. Later we went over to sextets instead of quintets, including in the package a deputy director for administrative matters. Experience showed that without such a manager if was difficult to cope with the vital problem of providing normal living facilities and amenities.

In my office at the Central Committee I had a big map of Kazakhstan on the wall. Just as in the old days at the front I used to mark the positions of army units, their zones of operation and lines of attack, so now I would mark on the map the deployment of hundreds of farms and operational centres. Circles indicated the main bases from which the offensive was to be launched: the towns nearest to the areas of cultivation, stations, and settlements lost in the boundless expanses of the steppe. Green-and-red flags indicated the old collective and state farms, which had also considerably expanded their crop area by driving into the virgin lands. And there were also red flags for the centres of the new state farms, which were then still to be built. In 1954, ninety red flags appeared on the map. By the beginning of 1956 there were 337!

People usually write in their memoirs how the directors of the state farms and their main specialists would drive out into the steppe with nothing but the order formalizing their appointment, a bank account number, and a rubber stamp in their pockets. They would arrive at their destination, drive some stakes in the ground for the name-board of the farm, and begin operations. . . . It's quite true that this is how things were done. But many of my old acquaintances, while paying tribute to the romantic side, forget one essential detail: they drove their stakes into the ground not at random, but at a strictly designated spot. And besides the orders and rubber stamps in their pockets, the state farm directors also had briefcases that contained maps showing the kinds of land allocated to the new farms and how they were to be used. There was romanticism galore in the virgin lands, and no shortage of difficulties. But the situation should not be oversimplified, as if people just roamed out into the steppe and started ploughing away with plenty of land all round to choose from.

Construction engineers have a concept—the zero cycle. It means the work connected with siting the building and laying out all its foundations and underground communications. This is a big, though outwardly unimpressive, job that has to be done before any building can be erected. In agriculture the "zero cycle", figuratively speaking, is the land-use surveying, all the work involved in allocating land to its various purposes. Land-use surveying provides a kind of general plan determining the outlines and character of the farm, the location and size of its fields, meadows and pastures, the siting of its buildings, its water supplies, and much else of vital importance for life and production.

At the republic's Central Committee an operational working group for the virgin lands took shape more or less automatically in the very first days. Later it was variously named: working, operational, some even called it the republic's virgin lands headquarters. Its activities were indeed reminiscent of a wartime headquarters. I was in charge of it. This group was not set up officially, it had no specially appointed members. All the people in it held their usual posts, but they were all directly connected with agriculture. Besides myself, the group included Fazil Karibzhanovich Karibzhanov, the Kazakh Central Committee secretary for agriculture; Andrei Konstantinovich Morozov and Vasily Andreevich Liventsov, heads of the Agricultural and State Farm Departments of the Central Committee; Grigory Andreevich Melnik, the republic's Minister of Agriculture; Mikhail Dmitrievich Vlasenko, the Minister for State Farms, and a number of other top officials. Of course, hundreds of people came to the republic's Central Committee on matters connected with the virgin lands, but the comrades I have named were the high command, the people who directed the whole enormous operation.

The allocation of land for ploughing was an urgent matter and unprecedented in scale. And if one had to say who was the first to go out into those boundless steppes, the answer would have to be that it was the scientists, the hydro-engineers, the botanists, the land-use surveyors, the agronomists. These are the people who, I feel, deserve first praise.

The fertile lands were not all located together. They had to be found, assessed, defined. It had to be decided which of them were

suitable for grain, and which for pastures. Nearly one-third of the
territory of Kazakhstan—100 million hectares—had to be studied
by the land-use surveyors. The Kazakh Republic's Academy of
Sciences alone formed and sent out into the steppe 69 expeditions
and groups. Specialists from academies, institutes and experimental
stations all over the country took part in studying and assessing the
land. Thousands of soil scientists, botanists, hydro-engineers, land-
use surveyors and agronomists from Russia, Kazakhstan, the
Ukraine and Byelorussia examined 178 of the republic's districts and
just to begin found 22.6 million hectares of land fit for the plough.
These lands, shown on detailed maps of the soil and vegetation, with
water supplies and raw material resources for the production of local
building materials precisely marked, were submitted first to the
district, and then to the regional and republican agencies.

I had a diploma in land-use surveying. So both in my capacity as
Central Committee secretary of such a large republic and as a
specialist in land surveying I was extremely interested in all this. The
scientists helped us to get our bearings quickly, identified the six
clearly defined economic zones in the republic, and gave clear
recommendations on where grain should be sown, where animal
breeding should be pursued, where the two should be combined,
and where irrigated farming should be developed.

At that time I struck up many friendships with my Kazakh comrades. I had taken a liking to the Kazakhs back in my wartime days.
They were very thorough, unassuming, dutiful and brave soldiers
and officers. In the lulls between the fighting they were always year-
ning for their homeland, for the spacious steppes with their waving
feather grass. Sometimes when I heard a Kazakh singing one of his
melodious and mournful songs, I would go up to him and ask,
"What are you singing about?"

"About the steppe. About the herd. I'm thinking about my
girl. . . . "

"A man can miss his girl and miss his home, but the steppe. . . .
You have the Ukrainian steppe here. Isn't it just as good?"

"Well, it's all right. It's just that our steppe is different."

And now, years later, I rejoice to see what fine Soviet people we have among the Kazakhs. There are top Party and managerial personnel, outstanding scientists, and gifted specialists in all fields, including culture and the arts.

I must say that the Kazakhs as a whole, the overwhelming majority, greeted the Party's decision to plough the feather-grass steppes with tremendous enthusiasm and approval. For the Kazakhs the cultivation of the virgin lands presented a complex problem. For centuries the Kazakh people had been involved in animal breeding, but now large numbers of them would have to break with the previous pattern of life in the steppes, become crop farmers, farm-machine operators, specialists in growing grain. But the local people had the wisdom and courage to take a most active and heroic part in the opening up of the virgin lands. The Kazakh people rose to the demands of history. They understood the needs of the whole country and showed their revolutionary, internationalist qualities.

My friendship with Dinmukhamed Akhmedovich Kunaev has lasted nearly a quarter of a century. In those days he was president of the Kazakh Republic's Academy of Sciences and, naturally enough, we got to know each other in the very first days of my stay in Alma-Ata. Educated as a mining engineer, a specialist in non-ferrous metals, he was not a man of narrow interests. He had a statesmanlike mind, could think broadly and boldly, and expressed some original and profound ideas about the huge resources and prospects of Kazakhstan. This calm, considerate, charming man also possessed a strong will and belief in Party principles. Soon he became chairman of the republic's Council of Ministers. Today he heads the Kazakhstan Party organisation and is a member of the Politburo of the CPSU Central Committee.

Dimash Akhmedovich (the friendly form of address adopted by everybody; no one uses his full name — Dinmukhamed) recommended to me as a consultant on the virgin lands the director of the Institute of Soil Science, Umirbek Uspanovich Uspanov. Under the

direction of this hard-working scientist the institute had ac-
cumulated vast amounts of information on the soil characteristics of
Kazakhstan, and its members made a considerable contribution to
everything concerning the siting of the new state farms.

I also have pleasant memories of Vasily Alexandrovich
Sheremetyev, head of the Department of Land-use Surveying of the
republic's Ministry of Agriculture. He was an extraordinary person.
Winter and summer he went about without a hat, in a soldier's
tunic, top-boots and always with an army-type field bag slung over
his shoulder. During the long years of his work in Kazakhstan he had
walked the length and breadth of the country and knew the steppes
blindfolded. He was absolutely indispensable when it came to choos-
ing the sites for the central buildings of the state farms. His field bag
struck me as a regular treasure trove, such as one reads about in
fairy-tales: from it he would produce maps, diagrams, notepads
with the names of hundreds of streams, landmarks, mountains,
sheltered spots, and also many names of the local inhabitants,
people who really knew the land. He always insisted on including
them in any commission for setting up new farms, and these old
Kazakh *aksakals** would gladly help us.

On learning that I had some experience of land-use surveying
Sheremetyev was absolutely delighted and began treating me as a
colleague, and sometimes even abused the situation by demanding
my intervention in minor matters that could have been decided
without me. But quite often intervention was needed. And
sometimes major intervention. One day he excitedly burst into my
office with an armful of land-use survey maps that had been sent to
him, if I remember rightly, from Kokchetav Region.

"Look what they're doing! They've tacked new areas onto the old
land without surveying the fields. I ring up the district centre and
get indignant and they calmly reply: what's all the fuss about? We've

aksakal village elder.

done this before, you know. As soon as spring comes, the snow will go away and we'll see at once where we ought to plough."

He was talking about the collective farms that had been allocated new land for cultivation. The people there had been working in the steppe for years and naturally considered themselves too knowledgeable to be interfered with. This attitude had to be overcome. We had to struggle against the oversimplified approach and demand that the selection of virgin land was always carried out on a strictly scientific basis.

Not only did one have to be able to take immediate action; one also had to go into things deeply and plan for the future. One could not grudge time or strength for the accomplishment of such a magnificent goal. Quite often I would stay on at the Central Committee late into the night, examining over and over again the maps and specifications of dozens of farms before they were finally accepted by the republican Council of Ministers and the central Ministry of Agriculture.

As most people know, 1954, if one takes into account all the considerable doubts that some people had, brought tremendous success in the cultivation of the virgin lands. For the country as a whole, instead of 13 million hectares, 19 million hectares came under the plough. And Kazakhstan also overfulfilled its cultivation plan. Need one say how much this inspired people and strengthened their confidence in the project. Having analysed our initial experiences and weighed the country's potential, the CPSU Central Committee and the USSR Council of Ministers passed a new decision "On further cultivation of the virgin and abandoned lands to increase grain production". Kazakhstan was given the task of setting up an additional 250 state farms.

The first ninety state farms founded in 1954 had been sited on the more convenient land, comparatively close to the railways and the available rivers. Now we had to drive deep into the boundless steppe. Our assignments became ever more complicated. For one thing it was more difficult to select land for ploughing. This gave rise to contradictions or, if you like, conflicting points of view.

I recall the battles that we had over two particular regions. The central Ministry of Agriculture held that nothing at all should be ploughed up in Aktyubinsk Region because the land there was supposed to be unsuitable for growing grain. On the other hand, when the local officials in Karaganda Region proposed setting up eighteen state farms on unproductive land, their "initiative" was supported without reservation. I called the minister in Moscow and said that this was an obvious mistake, but he described the Karaganda people as patriots and pace-setters and at the same time, evidently in the heat of the moment, accused the leaders of the northern regions, where the reserves of virgin land were in fact rather small, of conservatism and other mortal sins.

Such verbal polemics, without figures, reasons and arguments, are quite useless, I flew out to Aktyubinsk Region, met the specialists there, and saw for myself that there were some fertile lands in the region. I insisted that an expedition of scientists be sent there immediately. They did their work thoroughly and honestly and discovered 1.7 million hectares of good ploughland. A visit to Karaganda also convinced me that we were right. Once again I was confirmed in my belief that agriculture demands a scientific, not voluntarist approach.

In Alma-Ata we held a meeting of the republic's regional Party committee secretaries and regional executive committee chairmen. The republican Central Committee specially brought up for discussion the results of the selection of land for the new state farms. In a concluding speech I said at the time (I quote from the minutes):

"We have done a tremendous amount of work on allocating land. Nearly 9 million hectares have been found and classified. But the work is not yet finished. On these grounds—in both the figurative and literal senses—arguments have arisen with the Ministry of Agriculture. But we will stick to our positions and we hope to defend them successfully. It seems to us that Karaganda has not yet sorted out its land resources. It has been proposed that eighteen state farms should be organised. This seems quite a lot. But the plan for their siting cannot be accepted, because unsuitable land has been chosen. At the same time, in a number of districts of the region that I have visited myself there are good lands where state farms should be built."

I write in such detail about the surveying of the steppe and the allocation of sites for the new farms because the "zero cycle" in the cultivation of the virgin lands was of tremendous importance. The fate of the land that was to be ploughed and our whole future there depended on it.

3.

The first spring season in the virgin lands have left various impressions on my memory — joy, triumph, intense strain, difficulties. The steppe turned out to be a tough nut to crack, tougher than it had seemed at first. First, the centuries-old turf with its tangle of wire-like roots was so firmly packed that it would scarcely yield to the plough. Another difficulty arose from the fact that in the Kazakh virgin lands there is practically no spring in the usual sense of the word. Winter turns almost immediately into summer. Fierce heat marches literally in the wake of the melting snows. In May there is practically no rain, the land dries out quickly and becomes rock-hard and doubly difficult to plough.

Everywhere the first furrows were cut with great celebrations and meetings. The first squares were also ploughed successfully. In the virgin lands they were of unusual size. Everywhere the surveyors gave the tractor teams equal portions of untouched steppe, two kilometres square, in other words, an area of 400 hectares.

"That's a nice little square for you, plenty of room to move in!" the tractor drivers would joke. "Just switch on your engine and keep going till the fuel runs out."

But soon they found that they had to stop more and more often. The engines stalled, the ploughshares broke, the frames bent. Only a leviathan like the S-80 could pull a five-furrow plough. The manoeuvrable but lightweight DT-54 and 'NATI' were not powerful enough for the virgin lands. Everywhere people began taking one or even two shares off their ploughs. This not only reduced their per-formance — it threatened the whole plan for cultivation of the virgin lands.

The pre-sowing treatment of the virgin soil was not an easy business either. It had to be gone over several times with disk ploughs, then with ducks-foot cultivators, then it had to be harrow-ed and rolled with water-filled rollers. And only after that could the seeders be sent into action. But even with all this the interval between the first breaking of the soil and sowing could not be more than four or five days. We knew that otherwise the soil would dry out. Once that happened there would be no point in sowing it.

I remember my first visit to the sowing, in Kustanai Region. N. S. Khrushchev had arrived. He was at Tobol station. There was to be a big conference there. It was held at the Maikul Stud Farm, one of those which was turning up virgin land. We all assembled in the farm director's office — P. K. Ponomarenko, myself, I. P. Khramkov, first secretary of the Kustanai Regional Party Commit-tee, I. G. Slazhnev, chairman of the Regional Executive Committee, M. G. Motoriko, director of the Kustanai Stud Farm (now Kazakhstan's Minister of Agriculture), scientists from the All-Union Institute for the Mechanisation of Agriculture, and others. There was much to discuss, but the key problem was the turning of the furrow slice.

We had had a lot of trouble with it. The ordinary plough would not lay the massive slice of turf cut by the coulters at the bottom of the furrow. The broken turf stuck out at all angles and did not get covered by the lumpy lower soil. It was very awkward to disk such a field. We decided to adjourn the conference and go and see what all this looked like in practice. So we drove out to one of the tractor teams.

The tractor drivers were jumpy, the work was going badly. No matter how they tried, the slice would not turn over completely. I went up to them, joined in the conversation, and asked what they thought could be done. They replied that the existing ploughs were no good. A different kind was needed.

"What kind?"

"We've been saying it for a long time, but what's the use!" one of the drivers exclaimed. "You've got to get them to make ploughs with digger and semi-digger mouldboards. And it has to be done at once."

When N. S. Khrushchev found out what the problem was he became very angry and attacked the scientists. Why hadn't they foreseen this? Surely there had been time to advise the factories about such ploughs? Action was taken and within a month the first of the new ploughs began arriving in the virgin lands.

But it was still a month we had to wait. The ploughing of the virgin lands was already in full swing and we had to think of a way of keeping up the pace that had been set. One evening I made my usual round of telephone calls to the state farms to find out how much had been ploughed and what difficulties they were having. I rang the Ordzhonikidze State Farm. Its director, F. P. Kukhtin, said that things were going well, but asked us to send him some spare ploughshares.

"The shares don't last five minutes. . . . But we're ploughing at full speed. Come and see for yourself."

I asked how the turf turned over into the furrow. "Fine," came the answer. "We're tucking it in like a baby."

The next morning a big party of us went out to the Ordzhonikidze Farm. S. V. Kalchenko, the Deputy Minister of State Farms for the USSR, joined us and then, at the district centre, we picked up M. G.

Roginets, a CPSU Central Committee representative in the virgin lands. I had known Mikhail Georgievich since my days in the Ukraine, where he had been first secretary of the Chernigov Regional Party Committee, just at the time when I was working in Dnepropetrovsk. I hadn't seen him since then and I was glad at this unexpected meeting. Subsequently, as first secretary of the Kokchetav Regional Party Committee, and later, as Minister of State Farms and Minister of Agriculture for Kazakhstan, he put a lot of work into developing the virgin lands.

During the journey to the farm it transpired that it was he who had suggested "one little thing", and now the ploughing of the virgin lands in the districts under his charge was going well. The scene in the fields was encouraging. The tractor drivers were keeping up a normal speed without any trouble and the ploughs were biting into the virgin soil with a pleasingly steady crunch and tear. How so?

"I said it was just a little thing," Roginets replied with a smile. "We take off only a thin layer of turf, just the top. Look, the coulters are angled to a depth of only seven centimetres, not eleven, as stated in the instructions. That's how we do it."

And sure enough, the coulters, as we then noticed, were cutting off a thin slice of turf, like the rind off a piece of bacon, and tossing it, grassy side down, to the bottom of the furrow. They really were "tucking it in like a baby". I felt I had to reproach Mikhail Georgievich and the people from the farm. Why had they kept quiet about it?

"Well, you could hardly make a hullabaloo over a little thing like that. I thought people would think of it themselves. It's not all that hard," Roginets replied.

"You thought of it," I said, "but you mustn't forget that the whole country has come to the virgin lands and a lot of the people here are very young. Anything useful that's been learnt by experience must be spread around quickly. Even some of the experienced ones might

have thought of it, but they might have been afraid to take the risk
of infringing instructions. That's so, isn't it, Stepan Vlasevich?"

"Yes, they might be afraid," Kalchenko responded.

"So send out an instruction. Wherever they're having trouble with
the turf, let them angle their coulters at seven centimetres instead of
eleven."

"I'll write it today."

All the way back, we kept pulling Roginets' leg, telling him that a
Ukrainian always likes to rip off as thick a slice of bacon as he can,
but he only took a thin one. We had never seen such a thing before.

A day later there was a meeting of the buro of the Kustanai
Regional Party Committee. Among other matters the question of
building roads in the virgin lands was discussed. The majority was in
favour of highways for motor transport. It might be dearer and take
longer but, with an eye to the long-term, it would be better to start
at once developing an extensive modern road network. Large grain
elevators were to be built simultaneously at the main junctions.
However, Khrushchev maintained that it would be more expedient
to build several narrow-gauge railways to which, he claimed, the
grain could be brought from the most distant districts. No
arguments against this idea were taken into consideration. So a
narrow-gauge line from Kustanai to Uritskoe was laid, and then
another, from Yesil to Turgai. This was a mistake. Neither of the
lines came up to expectations as a means of transporting grain and
both were soon dismantled.

I cite this fact not to show that a Party and state functionary must
be at the same time a transport expert, an economist, an engineer
and so on. He does not have to be all these things, but he must
master the laws of general development and must also rely on concrete scientific and practical knowledge. And in any event he should
never regard himself as the sole and incontrovertible authority in all
fields of human endeavour.

Modern economics, politics, life in our society are so complex that
they will yield only to powerful collective reasoning. One must listen

to all that the experts and scientists have to say, and not only to those of one trend or school. One must consult people, so as to avoid any "chopping and changing", any hasty, ill-considered, voluntaristic decisions. These are particularly dangerous when a whole geographical area is being developed economically, socially and culturally, when it is a matter of the long-term policies to be adopted there.

From Kustanai I set out on a trip round the virgin land regions. Sowing was in progress everywhere.

At Yesil and Atbasar stations I encountered a genuine babel. The stations just could not cope with the amount of freight that was coming in. Even in those days Yesil was known as the gateway to the virgin lands, although it was only a tiny little station amid the vastness of the steppe. Massive quantities of freight were also arriving at the district centre of Atbasar. The little old township, dusty and open to every wind that blew, with its squat houses and stunted vegetation, was receiving trains loaded with machinery, timber, cement, prefabricated housing, field-camp wagons, metal, petrol, seed, food and merchandise, and not only for its own virgin land farms, but for the three adjoining districts as well. The whole population of the town had been mobilised to get the trains unloaded.

Members of the Party district committee buro, functionaries of the district executive committee, and Komsomol activists were on duty round the clock at the station, meeting the trains, directing the unloading, receiving the newcomers and trying to billet them in the homes of the local people. I say "trying" because the new arrivals did not want to be held up for a minute. They were eager to get out into the steppe and would go around shouting amid the general uproar the names of their farms: "Marinovsky! Atbasarsky! Dnepropetrovsky! Baumansky!" It had to be explained to them that the first parties had already been sent to the state farms, that they were already ploughing and sowing out there, and building accommodation for the reinforcements. Until there was somewhere to live, it was no use sending any more newcomers. We also explained that the rivers were in flood and to make the journey now would be simply dangerous. But arguments were of no avail. Placards were waved above the heads of the milling crowds: "All for the state farm!", "Off to the virgin lands!"

To the farms situated, like Atbasar, on the right bank of the Ishim river, machinery and people were still being dispatched in tractor and truck convoys. But some of the machinery, earmarked for the half of the district on the left bank, was held up by the spring floods. It would have been a sin to leave it standing idle, and so the local authorities decided to use it temporarily on the collective and state farms and tractor stations on the right bank. But suddenly one of the tractor teams disappeared.

It turned out that the leader of the team, Vladimir Chekalin, having heard about this decision, had roused his lads during the night and gone off with the tractors. These lads were bound for the "Red Dawn" Collective Farm on a Komsomol assignment. They had formed themselves into a team before they had left and were travelling with their tractors. Vasily Filippovich Makarin, the district Party secretary, set out in pursuit of the "runaways". On the bank of the Ishim he found the tractors and Chekalin himself, all alone.

"Where are the others?"

"They'll be here in a minute."

"Who gave you permission to break discipline like this?"

"We're not breaking discipline. Who are the tractors intended for? The 'Red Dawn' Collective Farm. And that's where they're going, as per instructions. We'll find a ford!"

Try as he might, the Party secretary could not make the team-leader see reason. He was adamant. Meanwhile the other tractor drivers came up to the bank of the river. Among them some white beards were to be seen — the local *aksakals*. When he heard what the argument was about, one of the old men turned to Makarin.

"Ah, secretary, why are you scolding the youngster? It's your own fault! Why didn't you send the machines earlier? Didn't you know there would be a big flood after all that snow?"

The Kazakhs showed the lads where the ford was and told them that at that spot the bed of the river was solid rock. The drivers soon dragged their tractors over to the other bank and put them to work on the collective farm the same day. The same ford was then used to send machinery across to the other state farms on the left bank, the Dnepropetrovsky, Marinovsky, and Baumansky.

Makarin was still excited and upset when he told me about this. After all, there had been an element of risk. And he was angry about the breach of discipline. But there had also been persistence, resourcefulness and daring. Incidentally, after the episode of the "runaways" a makeshift crossing was arranged. The people of Atbasar launched all their boats and two ferries were put together, and spring and summer they carried people, trucks, machinery, fuel and food across the river. This was also an example of true frontline resourcefulness. And I encountered so many similar examples in the virgin lands in those years that I could not possibly tell about them all here.

From Atbasar I drove on with Makarin. We took our time, visiting one farm after another, going from team to team. It was the first time I had seen the Kazakh steppe in the spring and I delighted in it. What an expanse! Even the sun must be tired by the time it has travelled from one horizon to the other. The vernal steppe was a blaze of colour. The blue gleam of the floodwaters. The fresh fragrant grass glistening in the sunshine. The flowering tulips. And here and there, all the way across this great sweep of green, lay the black squares of land, ploughed for the first time.

But on that wonderful sunny day I was beset by a worrying thought. In the course of my observations I had noticed that the squares of newly ploughed land were not being sown. The seeders were working only on the old ploughland. I recalled local people telling me that it had always been so; they sowed only in the second

year. I did not hurry to ask questions. But in one team I did ask a
local man, not a newly arrived tractor driver, "When are you going
to sow the virgin land? In June?"

"Sow in June?" he repeated in surprise. "We'd be a laughing-
stock. We have a saying down here: you might as well spit at a dune
as sow in June."

Makarin was silent on the way back to Atbasar.

"Isn't it time you made a report?" I said.

"What is there to report? You've seen for yourself."

It turned out that no one intended to sow this spring in Atbasar
District. Why? Makarin explained: it was an old custom that any
newly ploughed land should be sowed only the following spring
because it was always ploughed late, never before June. But why
late? Because before this the peasant was busy with his sowing. He
couldn't manage both jobs at once, sowing and ploughing. And by
the time he got around to the virgin land there was no sense in sowing. The earth waited for the next spring and only then did it yield
its first and usually good harvest. Hence the long-standing traditions, the accepted notions and ingrained prejudices. The Atbasar
people had debated the matter at great length and decided not to
sow in the first year.

I must admit that this was far from a new subject. Behind me I
had the advice of serious scientists. I had been through mountains of
data provided by expeditions that had begun to investigate the
virgin lands long ago. I shall have more to say about that later. For
the next, the 1955 harvest we planned to plough up as much land as
possible in June, because late summer or autumn ploughing both of
virgin land and winter fallow was just as undesirable in these parts as
June sowing. This had been proved by scientists and provided for in
our plans. But that first spring we were ploughing virgin land in
April and May, and not for next year's harvest, but for this year's!

People would have to be persuaded. We drove back to town, each
thinking his own thoughts. I had supper with Makarin at his home.
We drank two toasts with our Siberian meat dumplings, a favourite

dish of mine, prepared by his wife Feodosia Kuzminichna: one to a successful start on the virgin lands, and the other to our hostess. That evening Vasily Filippovich was tireless in asking all kinds of questions.

"Are you really convinced that this land will become one of the country's biggest granaries?"

"You have your doubts, do you?"

"We've had such a struggle with this land . . . "

"I'm not only convinced, Vasily Filippovich, I am proud to be involved in the project."

I understood this man well, I knew his state of mind. He was one of the old local functionaries that we, despite the radically changed scale of work, had decided to keep on at their former posts. And we had not been mistaken. The big changes put them at a loss only briefly. Makarin was one of thousands of district Party committee secretaries, those great workers who carry the main burden of the really difficult Party work, the work at grass-roots level. He had been living and working in one of the quietest little towns you could imagine, buried in the remote sun-scorched steppe, and his life had rolled by at a gentle, steady pace. But then came 1954 and the town became the epicentre of the virgin lands campaign, and in full view of the whole country. To Makarin's credit it can be said that he possessed that peasant thoroughness and the kind of mind that gets to the bottom of things and enables a man to acquire a deep faith in a new cause and to give himself up to it entirely with all the remarkable strength of his character.

The next morning, at my request, he assembled the state farm directors A. V. Zaudalov, I. G. Likhobaba and G. Y. Tutikov at the district Party committee office. The chairman of the district executive committee S. K. Galushchak, his deputy Rakhim Kaisarin and other officials were also there. Once again we went over everything. I listened attentively to everyone's opinion, and then in conclusion said:

"It's a good thing that you are adopting a thorough and cautious attitude to this great project. But let's go into what the argument is really about. Could the private peasant farmer, even if he was, as they say, in good fettle, work the virgin land as quickly as we can now? Of course not! With a wooden plough or, at best, a drill plough he could plough up his own patch of land as early as May, but then he simply didn't have the means to cultivate it. So he would wait for nearly a year, or even more, until the sods crumbled by themselves under the influence of the sun, water and frost. Should we take this peasant as our standard and take his bitter and unavoidable experience as our guide? I think not. With the machinery we have today we can make the upturned soil soft, porous and ready to receive the seed within two or three days. And we can reap the reward of our labours the very same year. So decide for yourselves what is the best thing to do."

"What is there to decide? I've been saying for a long time we ought to sow!" Zaudalov responded warmly.

"Well, sow then."

"But you see, it's not that anyone's preventing us or forbidding us. But the locals say: watch out or you'll come a cropper. You're not a local man and you don't know the soil. That's bound to put doubts into your head."

"We'll sow everything we've ploughed to date," Makarin assured me. "You've convinced us. It looks as if we thought ourselves into a muddle."

"All right then, but remember another thing," I added. "The arguments that were brought up here were agronomic and technical, and nothing was said about the political side of the question. But what we also have to consider is not just the feasibility but the necessity of sowing this spring and not later. And it's not just an economic necessity. It's a matter of politics. We want to let the whole world know, once again, that we communists can accomplish great things quickly. And besides, it's important for morale that every worker in the virgin lands should see the fruits of his labour this year."

4.

Sometimes people ask who fathered the idea of cultivating the virgin lands. I maintain that this question is wrong in its very assumption. It implies an attempt to attribute an outstanding achievement of our Party and people to the "vision" and will of one man.

The opening up of the virgin lands was a splendid idea conceived by the Communist Party, the realization of which almost instantly, if one uses the time-scale of history, helped to turn the country's lifeless and remote, but fertile eastern steppes into a land with a developed economy and flourishing culture.

The settlement of the vast expanses of Kazakhstan, Western Siberia and Russia's Far East by impoverished peasants from European Russia began, as we know, in the nineteenth century. It received a big boost with the opening of the Trans-Siberian Railway. But we also know what happened later. Millions of the dispossessed, landless, starving peasants of tsarist Russia headed eastwards with their families to the "promised land" in the desperate hope of finding land and happiness there. They travelled in crowded goods vans, two-wheeled carts and wagons. Thousands of these would-be settlers died on the road, exhausted by the long arduous journey, hunger and disease. Art and history have left us many testimonies to that dramatic epic. Take, for instance, the painting "Death of a Settler" by Sergei Ivanov. Way out in the remote steppe, on the road to a destination he will never reach, the head of a peasant family, its bread-winner, dies. What will happen to his widow, to the children? This is the painful question we ask ourselves when viewing that famous painting.

But even those who arrived safely on land that had never known the plough found themselves in desperate straits. They entered into single-handed combat with the wild and pitiless steppe. There was nowhere to live, no roads, no water, no help from anywhere. A skinny nag with a wooden or at best an iron plough were all the "mechanical means" they had.

The "opening up of the virgin lands" in pre-revolutionary times assumed the magnitude of a national disaster. The heartless, inhuman attitude of the tsarist authorities to the settlers was indignantly described by Chekhov, Korolenko and Uspensky. In his essays *Travels among the Settlers* Gleb Uspensky painted a typical picture of what he saw in one of the settlements.

"Black heaps of something that looks like piled peat or dried dung, not very large, scattered here and there and suggesting nothing that bears the slightest resemblance to human habitation; not a single human being anywhere to be seen, and not the slightest possibility of imagining that people could live here. And yet live they do. . . . "

We encountered the ruins of these "black heaps" — earthen dwellings — here and there in the steppe and they always evoked sad thoughts about the misfortunes of those first settlers in the virgin lands.

In the face of such unbearable conditions the peasants took flight back to Russia, to the Ukraine and Byelorussia — into the arms of a no less bitter fate. With fierce anger Lenin branded the policy of the tsarist government towards the settlers. He wrote: "It is the poorest who return to Russia, the most unfortunate, those who have lost everything and are bitterly angry. The land question must have become acute indeed in Siberia if it has become impossible, despite the desperate efforts of the government, to accommodate hundreds of thousands of settlers." And in another article: "This gigantic wave of returning settlers reveals the desperate plight, ruin and destitution of the peasants who sold everything in order to go to

Siberia, and who are now forced to come back from Siberia completely ruined."

In an attempt to justify the actions of the government, to smooth over the appalling impression given by the migration from west to east and back again of huge masses of desperate people, bourgeois students of the question invoked the theory that all the blame lay with the eastern steppelands themselves. The land, they maintained, was barren and unusable because of its natural features. But was there anyone in Russia who did not know that this was a slander of the rich virgin steppes that had been building up their fertility for centuries?

"The soil here is good for grain, vegetables and cattle," wrote S. U. Remezov, the author of *A Sketch-Book of Siberia*, about Siberia and Northern Kazakhstan, back in the eighteenth century. Ridiculing the inventions of the pseudo-scientists, Lenin wrote more than once: "There is still vacant land . . . excellent land, which should be opened up!" In Volume 13 of his *Collected Works* I found an amazingly profound observation. He writes that this land is unsuitable "not so much because of its *natural* properties . . . but because of the *social* conditions on the land . . . which doom agricultural techniques to stagnation and the population to rightlessness, oppression, ignorance, and helplessness. . . ."

The October Revolution fundamentally changed the "social conditions" of agriculture and thus created opportunities for making use of new land everywhere—in Western Siberia and Northern Kazakhstan, in the Volga area and the North Caucasus, in the Urals and the Far East. By 1940 the country's crop area had grown by 32.4 million hectares compared with 1913. The next stage in the cultivation of the USSR's land reserves was launched in the mid-fifties, when the urgent need for grain from the virgin lands coincided with a real opportunity to fulfil this historic mission.

The Party had been long preparing to launch this major advance into the new lands. In the late twenties N. M. Tulaikov, a scientist of world renown, who had had the vision to see that the creation of

was so thoroughly discussed. I
le involving Kliment Voroshilov.
gular trips round the agricultural
lmost despondent. Hearing that
n lands was being discussed, and
re amounts of money, manpower
"And in some Smolensk villages
oughs themselves. . . . "
e for the Party. It was only eight
re still bleeding. The fascists had
lages, sacked 98,000 collective
n away 17 million head of cattle
hat had not suffered enemy oc-
cal base of the tractor stations,
badly crippled. The machines
were past repair, the fields were
ll, there was a universal shortage
rivers, combine operators, truck
agronomists had been killed in

war level of agricultural output
de was still in need of assistance.
growing requirements of the
lustry for raw materials.
Committee plenum endorsed a
l to eliminate defects in the
r then, in view of the difficult
nd material, technical and man-
ed that all our strength be chan-
ning areas, so as to receive the

ugh designed to boost all bran-
d not ensure immediate success.
in objective — grain production.

large mechanised farms would offer the prospect of taming the
virgin lands, organised the first expedition to make an accurate
survey of usable land in the country's eastern regions. He wrote
about the success of the expedition in articles and in a memorandum to the Central Committee. In 1930, the 16th Party Congress — incidentally Tulaikov was admitted to the Party as a probationary member at this congress — debated the question of
expanding grain farming in the eastern regions. The Party's position
was clearly expounded in the report on "The collective farm movement and the intensified development of agriculture", prepared by
the Agricultural Department of the Central Committee. Here is an
excerpt from this interesting and far-sighted document:

"With wheat we shall go where more valuable crops cannot grow
and where the tractor can work twenty-four hours a day. According
to the calculations of Professor Tulaikov, a new probationary
member of the Party and one of the world's leading experts on
dryland farming, there are in Kazakhstan from 50 to 55 million hectares that could be considered suitable for sowing, of which nearly
36 million lie in the northern districts adjoining Siberia and the
Urals: Aktyubinsk, Kustanai, Petropavlovsk, Akmolinsk, Pavlodar
and Semipalatinsk. Here wheat crops occupy only five per cent of
the whole arable area.

"How do we intend solving this problem? It must be borne in
mind that the wheat problem will have to be solved in areas of very
low population density, in areas where the terrain will allow the
tractor and the combine to be used with maximum efficiency. . . . It
will take approximately 700,000 to one million horsepower to bring
an additional 20 to 25 million hectares under wheat. This we can
and should undertake!

"The organisational key to this problem is the minimal use of personnel and animals, so that large reserves do not have to be kept
there to safeguard against harvest failure. Besides complete
mechanisation, there must be a full work-load for the tractors, for

every machine, every person. The basic assumption must be th
one person should service 200 hectares.''

These proposals were adopted by the congress and supported a
approved by the people. The central and local press wrote a lot
the time about the need to open up the virgin lands. The Ministry
Agriculture began setting up the first grain-growing state farms
Kazakhstan and Siberia. Their experience helped us later, wh
organising the general advance into the virgin lands. It will be rea
ly understood, however, that in those years the country could not
send enough machinery into the vast expanses of the steppe. Th
came the war. But the idea of a general opening up of the virgin a
abandoned lands did not die. Like the soil itself, it waited for
hour of destiny.

In 1974, in a speech at a conference in Alma-Ata to mark t
20th anniversary of the opening up of the virgin lands, I said th
the true significance of historical events and major political d
cisions does not usually reveal itself at once, but only much late
when it becomes possible to compare the intent with the res
achieved, to evaluate the actual effect of these events and decisid
on this or that aspect of life. Historical distance tones down t
details and brings out the salient, fundamental features. And t
main thing about the virgin lands project is that in 1954 the Pa
set an extremely important and urgent national economic task. A
this was fully understood and appreciated by the Soviet people.

Let us recall the situation in the early fifties. The grain situati
in those years gave serious cause for concern. The country's avera
grain yield was not more than nine centners per hectare. In 19
only a little over 31 million tons of grain were laid in, as against t
32 million tons that were consumed. This meant that we had
draw on state reserves.

Basic, decisive and, above all, urgent measures were required
remedy the situation. Thus the Party, while not diverting its atte
tion from the problem of increasing the yield in the old agricultur
regions, spotlighted the task of achieving a significant and rapid e

This is why the gigantic proj
remember being told of one epis
He had returned from one of his
regions. He came back worried,
the question of opening up the vi
realising that this would require
and machinery, he remarked sad
the people are still pulling their

It was by no means an easy ch
years since the war. The wounds
burned and destroyed 70,000
farms and 1,876 state farms, dri
and 7 million horses. In the are
cupation, the material and tech
and state and collective farms
had been worked for years till th
in a state of neglect. And worst o
of manpower—millions of tracto
drivers, mechanics, engineers a
the war.

After tremendous effort the p
had been restored, but the count
Agriculture was not satisfying
population for food, or those of

The September 1953 Centra
wide-ranging programme desig
management of agriculture. Su
position with regard to ready cas
power resources, logic itself dema
neled into the traditional crop-
maximum return.

But the Party's programme,
ches of agriculture, did not and c
This was particularly true of the

It is usually a lengthy process to obtain increased returns in field cropping, and plant growing is usually a lengthy process. So, even if it involved a risk, we had to win time by boldly channeling part of our funds and resources into the virgin lands, promising as they did a solid boost to the country's badly strained grain balance within a single season. The first thirteen million hectares of virgin land earmarked for cultivation in 1954 could, if all went well, put an additional thirteen to fifteen million tonnes of marketable grain in our granaries that very autumn. And this was the course the Party took. In doing so it gained both the tactical advantage of an immediate and tangible result in the form of grain, and the strategic advantage which lay in the fact that we were going out to the virgin lands not lightly equipped for "snatching" their riches, for skimming the cream of their fertility and going home again, but to stay there for a long time to come.

Incidentally, Kliment Voroshilov was among those who knew how to judge whether a major state undertaking was timely or premature. He came out in favour of the virgin lands and later, on visiting Kazakhstan and seeing the boundless wheatfields, he said to me joyfully, "What a good thing we came here! The help that the Byelorussian, Smolensk and Vologda people need is ripening here on these broad expanses. And it's coming in an express ambulance. Why, we should paint yellow crosses on the trucks carrying the virgin land grain to match the colour of the wheat. . . . It's a great help to us, a great help!"

But all that came later. At this time, in 1953-54, the debate continued. One of the most formidable objections was: how could one possibly contemplate moving such a huge armada into absolutely bare and uninhabited steppe without any ancillary services? No, first of all one must build settlements, schools, hospitals, roads, repair factories and shops, elevators, and only then bring in the machines and personnel.

What answer could one give to that? Of course, it would have been good to have all these things. But those who put the question in that way did not understand the main thing—grain was needed from the virgin lands at once! We were going there to settle the land, make it habitable, and take the grain all in one operation. In building socialism Soviet people have often had to start with next to nothing in order to win time. The Party openly told those it called upon to join the project: it's going to be difficult, very difficult; it will be a battle and any battle demands heroism. And hundreds of thousands of patriots consciously took the task on.

Traditionally, the Party never takes major, fundamental decisions without consulting the people. And this was no exception. At the end of 1953 and the beginning of 1954, in the hundreds of meetings and conferences that were held in the territories and regions of the Russian Federation, Kazakhstan and other republics it was evident that Party members as well as the broad mass of the people approved and supported the Party's idea of opening up the virgin and abandoned lands.

Of course, in the places where the battle for the virgin lands was to actually take place there was also controversy and doubt. But there are doubts and doubts. When people realised that the Party was not just planning a quick raid into the virgin lands, but that it had worked out and prepared a large-scale national economic programme, they supported it without hesitation. The story told by a man I have already mentioned in these notes, V. F. Makarin, first secretary of the Atbasar District Party Committee, who became a Hero of Socialist Labour in the virgin lands, is characteristic. This is what he wrote about his misgivings in those days:

"Now that many years have passed and much has been forgotten, one could brag a little and say that all of us who were in one way or another drawn into the orbit of the virgin lands were prepared, like cavalrymen with bared sabres, to charge into the attack on the silent steppe and take it by storm. But this would be quite contrary to the truth. To be quite honest, I have to admit that when we learned what was in store for the people of Atbasar, we in the district leadership were, to put it mildly, taken aback. And this is not so hard to

Among virgin landers, winter.

A barber's shop run by the settlers, 1955.

Cooking breakfast on makeshift stoves.

May 1954: erecting a tent.

Young Communist League members and their friends, leaving Leningrad for the virgin lands, 1955.

Kartauzov (*left*) and Ivanov (*right*): "Their fates have been similar and they are both heroes of our nation. That is a coincidence which I would describe as symbolic. Not for nothing has the term 'Virgin Land' become for us a symbol of courage."

understand. We, who had been born, had grown up and worked all our lives in these parts, knew what the virgin land was like. We knew how grudgingly it yielded to the peasant. It was no accident that in more than a hundred years the Atbasar peasants had been able to plough only 100,000 hectares of virgin land and had sowed only a third of it, and this only in the best, most favourable years. But now within the next two years our district was to open up nearly half a million hectares, plough nearly the whole steppe and make it bear grain! That was something to think about. . . . It was not that we had the slightest doubt that the country would provide us with enough machines. By that time we had a developed industry and massive economic resources. But who, may I ask, was going to operate the machines? The machine has not yet been invented that can by itself, without human participation, plough, sow and harvest grain, and turn it into loaves. Some people may accuse me of exaggeration, but I am speaking of what it was really like in those days. We were embarking on a great and unknown undertaking and it contained a considerable element of risk."

My old acquaintance Vasily Filippovich Makarin was right. There was a risk, and the district Party committee secretary had every reason to ponder on how best to perform the task set by the Party. In fact, he was bound to. It was also right that the district committee frequently called together all the local activists, and that they argued till they were hoarse, suggesting various courses of action.

"But our doubts", Makarin concludes, "were soon dispelled. The Party had everything worked out. It was relying on the people's boundless trust, on their high civic awareness and enthusiasm. The machinery soon began flowing into our district, thousands of letters arrived from young people asking for the addresses of collective and state farms that needed help, hundreds of specialists, splendid technical experts, came out to us in response to the Party's appeal. And so the unprecedented, heroic task began.

5.

In old dictionaries you will find the term "virgin land", but not "virgin lander". It was coined in the fifties, just as the term "collective farmer" was coined during collectivisation. The very concept of virgin land lost its purely agricultural connotation. It became a social term, implying a high sense of civic responsibility and Soviet patriotism. The virgin lander is a historic figure and represents a heroic age. And the word connotes the special character shaped by the demands of that time.

One day, when I arrived at a state farm in Kustanai Region where only one small house was ready for newcomers and people were still living in tents and dug-outs, I learned that the best room had been given to a young couple who had just had a son. Everyone was celebrating the occasion and the happy father told me: "We've only just arrived, but we already think of ourselves as native virgin landers."

"No," I replied, "the only native virgin lander on this whole farm is the boy that has just been born here. You still haven't taken root. I don't think it'll happen so quickly nor will it be easy."

I recall the talks I had long ago in Tselinograd Region and in Atbasar District—first in spring, and then in autumn. The second time around everything had changed. During the first spring in the virgin lands I heard complaints from the farm directors that by no means all the newcomers intended to stay. A. V. Zaudalov, the director of the Marinovsky State Farm, told me, "In one way, the people are a mixed lot, but in another, they're like an army—all young people, and here today, gone tomorrow."

"Yes, it's a problem," I agreed. "The young are always out for adventure. In a year or two some of them will begin to leave. You can see for yourself, most of them just want to live in tents. They want it rough, they want a challenge. They'll do all the spade-work, then get bored and take off."

"So what can we do?"

"Try to think how you can keep people on the farm. I can think of two ways of doing it. First, invite some girls here. Dairy-workers, seeder operators, telephonists, cooks, doctors, teachers. There's plenty of work for them here already, and there'll be plenty more tomorrow. Invite the girls and many of the lads will stay on for good. And the second way is to invite family people. But you'll have to create normal conditions for them first. That's how we'll settle this land."

What we were really talking about was planning for human happiness. Everyone needs a home, love, children. Neither the state nor society can find everybody their "chosen one", as they used to say in the old days, but we must try to see to it that there are no purely "male" regions or "female" towns. And if the demographic problems are dealt with competently, the young people will find each other and be happy. And happy they must be because without that the country cannot prosper.

Atbasar District soon took the initiative in inviting young women to the virgin lands. On returning to Alma-Ata on 17 July 1954, I was pleased to read in *Pravda* a letter from some young women from the Marinovsky State Farm, Raisa Yemelyanova, Alexandra Zamchy, Yelena Kleshnya, Valentina Nepochatova, Polina Pashkova and Lyudmila Semenova, appealing to girls and women throughout the country to come to the virgin lands. The response was tremendous. When I returned to Atbasar in the autumn, at harvest-time, I met Zaudalov again. He was both glad and extremely worried.

"What's up?" I asked.

"Well, for goodness sake, Leonid Ilyich! It seems I'm not the director here any more, but the head postman. . . . The farm has been getting thousands of letters from girls. They're all ready for the road, they all want to come here and nowhere else! Things ought to be regulated somehow. There are plenty of other farms. Otherwise this one will be more like a fair for brides than a state farm!"

The "girl invasion" caused a good many headaches. But life in the virgin lands changed literally before our eyes. More and more rapidly it stopped being "army" or "campaign" life and acquired the normal comforts. And today, no matter where I go in the new lands, I always meet workers who were born there. Life in those parts has put down deep and strong roots.

Zhansultan Demeev, a Hero of Socialist Labour, goes out to the fields with his son, Mirash Demeev. The soil here knows not only the famous pioneer virgin landers, Mikhail Dovzhik and Vladimir Dityuk, but also their sons, those fine farmers Vladimir Dovzhik and Grigory Dityuk, who were born here. More than once I have visited the Zhdanov State Farm, in the North Kazakhstan Region, and met its director Mark Pavlovich Nikolenko. When this veteran retired, the directorship of the farm was taken over by his son—Vladimir Markovich Nikolenko. Amangeldy Isakov, a combine operator on the Lenin State Farm, Karasu District, Kustanai Region, became a Hero of Socialist Labour in the virgin lands. And today his son Vladimir is the chief agronomist of the Koibagar State Farm in the same district. Ivan Grigorevich Kosmych, a combine operator on the Samara State Farm, Tselinograd Region, has founded a real farming family: he has nine sons who work with him, growing and harvesting the grain! I could quote any number of such examples. Everything went according to plan: the new lands were brought into cultivation, and people took to living there.

The tent used by M. E. Dovzhik's team in the virgin lands has long been on display in the Museum of the Revolution in Moscow. Hundreds of steppeland towns have grown up where those tents and dugouts once stood. Today 1,200,000 people live and work on the farms in the virgin land districts of Kazakhstan. These places have become just as settled as any other economic area in the country.

Photographs of the first years in the new lands revive many memories. Bare steppe, tractor columns, stakes bearing the names of farms, tents, dug-outs, crowded trailers and mud huts with flat roofs, known as "sailors' caps". People used to huddle together in these dwellings by the dim light of lanterns and oil lamps. Everything was temporary, comfortless, rough and ready. But look at their faces—how merry, how joyful they are. Every smile, every gesture conveys confidence and optimism. All of us who were working in the virgin lands in those days felt this optimism, the feeling of people aware of their own strength. And how impressive the steppe was once we had awakened it to life! Everything was on the move, converging on this front-line area, just like before a big offensive. Anyone who came to the virgin lands in those days could not help feeling involved in its demands and aspirations.

No one denies that some people left the virgin lands. Some were just passing through, self-seekers who made impossible demands and refused to consider anything but their own interests. They were aptly nicknamed "passers-through". I ran into some of them during my very first trip round Northern Kazakhstan. In the early spring of 1954, at Tobol station, I had scarcely stepped out of the train when a loud-voiced young man bounced up to me out of the crowd and literally bombarded me with questions. Where had they been brought to? Why had they been talked into coming here? Where was the accommodation, the good wages, the warm clothing? Only a marmot in its hole could live in this steppe!

I listened patiently, then said that this was why they had been invited, to make these places habitable. But the fellow was not to be placated. He showed me his flimsy jacket and demanded to be given a sheepskin immediately. Clearly this was not the kind of person you could argue with—you can always sense that type at once—and I had to cut him short.

"Did you expect to find everything ready and waiting for you? What was the idea of coming here just in a jacket and cap? The virgin lands don't need people like you!"

"Ah, it's always the same", he replied on a less strident note, "when you start demanding your legitimate rights."

"No, lad," I said, "your demands might be legitimate a month from now, perhaps two or three, and even then only partly so. They won't be fully legitimate for at least a year. At the moment there are just as many claims that can be made on you. What are you here for? We were relying on you, and now we shall have to chase around for a replacement. But you can be quite sure that we will find one."

As far as I can remember this lad was in a group from the town of Shuya. Of course, he was an exception to the rule. Shuya sent us some very good workers. They named a farm in the Turgai steppe "Shuisky", after their home-town, and it became one of the best in the virgin lands.

There were problems; there is no point concealing the fact. Through those heroic years our people sacrificed a lot in the name of the future. They endured many grave ordeals. At various stages they were short of everything—nails and kerosene, shoes and the simplest kinds of cloth, a roof over their heads, even bread. But the Party always told the people openly: we will overcome the difficulties and shortages by united, determined effort and our life will gradually get better and better. And each year it did get better, despite the fact that the country had to face many new trials.

Of course, people who have had to bear the hardships that have come with certain periods of our history have not found life easy. Sometimes it was desperately hard. Every generation of Soviet people has experienced difficulties. No people on earth has endured such trials as ours. But look at our life as a whole. It has been getting better all the time. No matter what the obstacles, we have always surmounted them. And our life today is as different from the past as a spaceship is from a peasant wagon.

But let's get back to the problems that we encountered in the new lands when they were being opened up. They were temporary, of course. Only the egotists who did not want to lift a finger for the common cause failed to realise that. For that kind of individual the people have the right phrase — they're only out for themselves.

But young folk one met who had simply lost their bearings in new surroundings were a different matter. It was enough to have a talk with them, to explain and persuade, and show a little fatherly kindness. Yes, winning with kindness was a term I often used when discussing these matters with the people in charge. A young man with no experience needs some strictness but he also needs kindness. In that spring of 1954 at Dzhaltyr station, near Tselinograd, I noticed a lad with a suitcase. He was obviously waiting for a train.

"You're not going home, are you?"

"Yes, I am."

"Rough, is it?"

"Yes. It seems to me now I've never known what sort of person I really am. I never thought I'd miss home so much. It's warm there. I can see the Sea of Azov from our window. The orchards are in bloom. Here it's just snowstorms and blizzards. And now these terrible winds. . . . "

I sat down beside him.

"It's always hard at first. But just think of the young men of your age fighting at the front. They missed their homes and mothers too, and they lived in dug-outs. And besides that, they were facing death. . . . Nothing big ever comes easy. It's no problem to grow an orchard in the Ukraine, but here in this steppe an orchard becomes something great. And yet in a year or two there will be villages and orchards here. The main thing is to have faith in yourself. You mustn't begin life with a retreat!"

That lad, I remember, did not get on the train. I saw him later in the back of a lorry. I never knew his name. Of course, he wouldn't be young now, but I think he is among those who decided to link their future with the feathergrass steppes.

"Human existence is impossible in the wilderness of the virgin lands," a bourgeois newspaper wrote in those days. "We can rest assured that the virgin lands will remain an undigested lump in the Russian stomach."

How many other scathing prophecies of that kind were to be heard in those days! And yet within three months of the arrival of the first trainloads of volunteers, the steppe was green with boundless fields of wheat. The republic's crop area was doubled, and that year reached 20 million hectares. And if, as those who wished us ill wrote, we were "not ready" for the virgin lands, how was it that we ploughed and sowed these lands? How was it that we received more than 22,000 new tractors and more than 10,000 new combines that year? How was it that we were sent thousands of trainloads of houses, timber, cement, merchandise, and food? No, this was well thought-out, a properly planned offensive. And the centuries-old fortress named the "virgin lands" fell not to a prolonged siege, but to a sudden onslaught, a heroic assault.

The question might be asked: but if these people went out into the steppe equipped with powerful machinery and feeling that they had the whole country, the whole people behind them, if even then they were being sung of as national heroes and from the outset began to reap the fruits of their enviable renown, aren't we exaggerating the significance of the term "virgin lander" and all it stands for? No we are not. These people really did achieve something great.

Heroism manifests itself in various ways. A man might rush into a burning house at the risk of his life but prove incapable of going on day after day at a monotonous job. There is the heroism of the moment. There is the heroism we find during grave periods in the lives of people, war being an example. And there is everyday heroism, when people consciously and voluntarily commit themselves to hardships which they know they could avoid elsewhere. I am of the opinion that the people working in the virgin lands showed themselves to be heroes. They stood up to all the difficulties of daily life in those early days and then for years worked on, patiently and steadfastly, making this far from gentle land a good place to live in.

During the celebrations of the 20th anniversary of the virgin lands I spoke in Alma-Ata about an amazing man — Ivan Ivanovich Ivanov. He was born in Leningrad. During the war while defending his native city, he was seriously wounded and lost both legs. After a long period of convalescence he arrived in Kazakhstan, and there he stayed. He adopted this country and the country adopted him. He developed into a fine machine operator and to his war medals were added awards for labour — two Orders of Lenin and a Hero's Gold Star.

The whole hall applauded. Then came other speakers, and one of them told what sounded to me like the same story. He, too, spoke of a communist, a Leningrader, a war veteran who had lost both legs, who had come to the virgin lands and become one of the best tractor drivers in the republic and a Hero of Socialist Labour. But in this story the man's name was Leonid Mikhailovich Kartauzov. . . . Again everyone began to clap and I wondered whether this was some coincidence. Or had I got the hero's name wrong? But no, that was impossible, I remembered him well.

During the interval I asked about Kartauzov and it turned out that there had been no mistake. Both Kartauzov and Ivanov work in the virgin lands, their fates have been similar and they are both heroes of our nation. That is a coincidence which I would describe as symbolic. Not for nothing has the term "virgin lander" become for us a symbol of courage.

In the course of my life I have often observed that in normal circumstances true heroes are, as a rule, modest and not very conspicuous people. They simply do their job. Such a man was Daniil Nesterenko, a tractor driver of the Dalny State Farm, Tselinograd Region. The name of the farm ("Distant") speaks for itself; it is situated in the remotest corner of the region. And this was where Nesterenko volunteered to go. The snowy winter was drawing to a close and the tractor team he worked in was in danger of being cut off from the farm centre and running out of fuel. The Zhanyspaika, an insignificant little river, might, so the local people said, burst its banks and flood the surrounding country. The tractors had to be driven across while it was still iced over. Nesterenko helped his workmates perform this rather risky operation, and only then set out in his own tractor. But the melting ice, already half under water, gave way. . . .

When his friends pulled him out they found a Hero of the Soviet Union's card in the dead man's pocket. Until then no one on the farm had known they had such a person working with them. It transpired that Daniil Nesterenko had won his award during the forcing of the Dnieper during the war. And this made his death doubly sad. I remember the Dnieper, I remember the heroes of that crossing under deadly fire. Surely a little steppeland river was no obstacle to such a veteran! But such tragic accidents do happen.

One detail struck me as particularly moving. In Nesterenko's tent his friends found some Ukrainian cherry saplings. He must have come to Kazakhstan to stay if he had brought these young trees with him to plant in the steppe. But he was not there to see them grow.

The winter of 1954 was a severe one, with unusually heavy snow and frost. Right from the start the virgin land put the newcomers to the test and hit out at them with its fierce, unfriendly temper. The biting winds howled incessantly and every journey across the steppe became exceptionally difficult and dangerous. And yet thousands of tractors and hundreds of convoys of trucks had to get through to farms that still had not been built, through the wind and snow and over country without roads.

Most of us can imagine what a snowstorm in the steppe is like from our childhood reading of Pushkin's *The Captain's Daughter.* I, myself, have seen how deceptive the steppe can be. One minute the frosty sky is blue from horizon to horizon and bright with sunshine; next minute you can't see a thing through the howling, whirling, whistling snowstorm. One small mistake, a mere mischance, an unexpected engine failure, and a man is left all alone in the steppe with no road to follow, in the bitter cold and pitch black.

I remember how shocked everyone was by the death of Vasily Raguzov, a correspondence-student at the Lvov Construction Institute. He had been one of the first to arrive at the Kiev State Farm and was working as a building foreman. A capable organiser and a good comrade, jolly and sociable by nature, he quickly won the respect and affection of his fellow pioneers. On one of those clear days Raguzov was with a convoy bringing prefabricated houses from the station for the state farm's first street. Suddenly they were hit by an exceptionally fierce blizzard that went on for several days. The convoy stopped. Vasily decided to go for help on foot. He set off alone, lost his way and perished. He was a brave man with tremendous willpower. Here is a letter that was found in his pocket.

"To the person who finds this notebook! Dear Friend, be so good as to pass on what is written here to Serafima Vasilevna Raguzova, Flat 1, 15 Goncharov St, Lvov.

"My dear Serafima! There's no need for tears. I know it will be hard for you but what can I do now that this has happened to me. There's nothing but steppe all round, it goes on forever. I've no idea where I'm going. The storm is nearly over, but there's no sign of the horizon that could give me my bearings. If I don't get back, bring up our sons to be decent human beings. Ah, life! How I long to live! Lots of kisses. Yours forever, Vasily."

Realizing that death was near, he wrote a postscript with numb, frozen fingers.

"To my sons Vladimir and Alexander Raguzov.

My dear children, Vovushka and Sashunka! I came out to the virgin lands so that our people would have a richer, better life. I want you to continue my work. The main thing in life is to be a human being. A big kiss for you, my dear ones. Your Dad."

It might seem that this letter is a purely personal one, just for his family. But it has become an appeal to all mankind. When I was shown the pages with their blurred letters and managed to read them, I felt a lump in my throat. I rang up the papers and suggested that, if they could obtain the wife's permission, they should publish this letter. When it was printed it evoked a response from tens of thousands of people all over the country. New parties of volunteers came to the virgin lands to complete the work begun by Vasily Raguzov and other brave people like him. The hill near which Vasily had died now bears his name.

The present-day map of Kazakhstan testifies to the fact that the virgin lands were indeed opened up by the whole country. Its geography is reflected in the names of the farms—"Moscow", "Leningrad", "Minsk", "Kiev", "Dnepropetrovsk", "Armavir", "Poltava", "Tagil", "Sochi", "Perm", "Yaroslavl", "Voronezh". . . . On many of the farms one met people of other nationalities besides the Kazakhs, the native inhabitants of the steppe. The virgin lands became a true school of internationalism, a depository of the wisdom and experience, the skills, the will to win of all the peoples of our country.

New lands are always pioneered by new people. But here there was something special. We had come a long way since the days of the first five-year plans, when the volunteers came to Magnitka, the Turksib railway, the Dnieper Dam or Komsomolsk-on-Amur with only saws and shovels. The prime need in the virgin lands was for tractor drivers, electricians, truck drivers, mechanics and builders, and people with these skills were sent to us from many republics, territories and regions of the USSR. They formed the backbone of the new economic units.

People raised grain on the land and the land raised people. Metaphorically speaking, the virgin lands yielded a rich harvest of hard workers, patriots, people of skill and dedication. But coming as they did from all parts of the country, with their own peculiarities, characters, experience and inclinations, they did not knit together automatically. And here I feel I must say a word about the organisational and ideological methods we had to evolve. Everything that the Party did in the virgin lands was an epic of innovation, and an extremely successful one.

In atmosphere it most nearly resembled the political work during a big offensive operation. For me those first months entailed endless journeys and hundreds of meetings and brief encounters when people could not be interrupted for too long and I, myself, was short of time. I always had to push on. I felt constantly drawn towards the "frontline". I wanted to go everywhere, to be in a dozen different places at once. That was, of course, impossible. But it did all work out somehow. The essence of Party political work at that time was to unite this huge mass of people and give them a concrete programme of action and a clear awareness of the common goal.

I remember how in my car or during long tramps across the steppe, at night in the tents and in the evening by the campfires I would repeat the same thing over and over again to the Party secretaries. The message ran approximately as follows: bring the Party members together more often; let them get to know each other, discuss the situation, weigh each other up. Then they will be able to lead.

"We have nowhere to hold Party meetings," I was told.

"But it's essential," I insisted.

"There's a bit too much criticism flying around," some would object. "We haven't got this, they haven't sent us that. . . . You know what it's like at the beginning."

"Never mind," I said. "Keeping quiet won't make things any better. When people get together, argue and bring it all out in the open, you'll soon find them offering a solution themselves. And the next meeting you must tell them what's been done. People have come here from all over the country and they're a very mixed bag—that's the main problem. But there is also an advantage. There's a real hard job to be done and it quickly shows what a man is made of."

That first spring all my energies were concentrated on swinging that enormous machine into motion and there was no time to stop and rest.

And then came the long-awaited and nevertheless unexpected bumper grain crop from the virgin lands.

6.

I shall never forget the first autumn in the virgin lands, the autumn of 1954. At a meeting at one of the state farms in Ruzaevka District, Kokchetav Region, they presented me with a sheaf of "akmolinka", virgin land wheat. I couldn't possibly express my feelings as I held that sheaf in my hands. Memories came flooding into my mind—the first ideas and plans, the sleepless nights, the arguments, the trainloads of people, the tractor columns battling their way across the roadless blizzard-swept expanses, the first campfires in the steppe, the first furrows. And here it was, before my eyes, a dream come true—the steppe, yellow with wheat from horizon to horizon. . . . I remembered the handful of pioneers, the very first virgin landers, who soon after the revolution had founded the farming communes in these parts. Referring to the workers of the Obukhov and Semyannikov factories who had decided to go to Kazakhstan, Lenin wrote in a note to the Minister for Agriculture: "Their initiative is excellent; support it in every way."

The first communes in the Ishim steppe had joyous names: "Ray of Revolution", "Light of Truth", "Road to the New Life". But how poorly equipped these small settlements on the virgin lands were. The "Ray of Revolution" Commune, for instance, had four bullocks, eleven cows, one reaper, one mower, four harrows, eight wagons, four houses and a barn. What willpower and faith in eventual victory was needed to be able to say: "You are going to yield to us, steppe! You will become our provider!" And now, instead of those tiny islands, there was a steppe-wide ocean of wheat. The old plain with its waving feather-grass was becoming one of the state's greatest granaries. This was the first return from the first year's work in the virgin lands.

The ocean of wheat rolled across the steppe, the wind rippled its heavy waves, the sun gilded them, and everyone was pleased and proud. But how much work was still needed to bring all that grain home!

Today the new lands of Kazakhstan have a massive system of large elevators and grain-storage sheds. But in those days the total storage capacity was no more than three million tons, including the primitive barns and various kinds of mud huts which the virgin landers that autumn dubbed "dog kennels". The grain had to be harvested, stored and delivered at all costs. A particularly difficult situation developed on the roads, at the stations and at the grain-transport terminals.

Let me describe just one episode. It happened when I flew into Atbasar with Nikolai Ivanovich Zhurin, first secretary of the Tselinograd Regional Party Committee. As soon as we landed, our hosts wanted to rush us off to the farms, to the fields, to give us the joy, as they put it, of seeing the harvest. But these invitations were just a bit too persistent and not a word was said about the local grain depot. Naturally we decided to see it first. Someone warned us, "You can't go there. The drivers will tear you to bits, honestly they will! There's a colossal jam of trucks. They have to wait two days to unload!"

"Well, that's not so terrible," I said. "We've just been at Koluton station. They're in real trouble there: grain galore and not enough trucks to carry it."

We drove up to the depot. It was a kilometre from the railway. It was a bright and clear autumn day. On the outskirts of the town, amid the scorched rust-brown steppe, hundreds of trucks loaded with grain were standing in a queue over a kilometre long. The depot itself was like a disturbed ant-hill. Clouds of dust rose over the grunting, snorting trucks as they tried to get through to the centre of the yard, to the great heaps of grain. From nearby came the clanging and hammering of a construction site, where a new elevator was being built. The old, rather small one was already full to overflowing. Hundreds of people were standing about with nothing to do. About twenty women were shovelling grain into sacks, which would then be carried into low mud huts where the seed grain was to be stored. The trucks were being unloaded entirely by hand, and only in two or three places.

I went up to one of them and scooped up a handful of grain. It was a delight to look at: the solid heavy seed shone like gold in my hands—a marvel!

We were at once besieged by the drivers. The uproar was unimaginable, it drowned out everything. The drivers shouted that they were being held up for days on end, they had to spend the night in their cabs, there was nowhere to get a bite, to wash off the dust. But this was nothing compared with the fact that in the steppe the grain was already mountains high. Out there in the open it would be ruined! I let them get it all off their chests, then said, "This is a fine way to welcome your guests."

I don't know whether it was my calm or perhaps the smile that did it, but the drivers fell silent: after all, a man deserves to be given a hearing.

"Don't get excited, comrades," I went on, not yet knowing myself what to do. "We'll think of something. I give you my word, we'll sort out this jam."

I had made a promise, but what was the answer to the problem? We walked round the depot, inspected the elevator that was being built and would not be ready until next autumn, and also had a look at the "dog kennels". I found myself constantly glancing at a large strip of wasteland between the depot and the station, the so-called "separation zone". It was cluttered with all kinds of rubbish—rusty scrap iron, chunks of ferro-concrete, refuse. It all lay chaotically amid the withered yellow weeds, coated with dust that had been accumulating for years.

"Who does this land belong to?"

"The railway."

I asked to see the chief of that section of the line. He quickly appeared and introduced himself as Baizak Permenovich Permenov. He turned out to be a sensible business-like man who knew his job and was also fond of a joke, for he added, "And please don't get the name wrong. A lot of people mistake me for Balzac. But I'm not a writer, I'm a railwayman. And not French either, but pure Kazakh."

The problem we had to solve was a difficult one. I asked if one of the old grain purchasers could be found.

"We don't even have to look for him," Permenov replied. "Here he is, standing right beside us — Nikanor Georgievich Simenkov. At the moment he's building the new elevator, but he used to be head of the regional procurement board. He's the expert around here."

We went into a huddle on the edge of the wasteland. I knew the district officials well, but the head of the storage depot, Povliyanenko, was new to me. I exchanged a few words with him and learned that he was a war veteran, ex-navy. But I put my first question to the railwayman.

"How many days would it take to clear this patch of wasteland and lay a branchline to it?"

Permenov made a calculation on a notepad and said, "A day for clearing and two days for laying the line."

"You're not asking for long enough. Let's say five days. . . . How much grain will the district be bringing in?"

Zhurin replied: "More than one district uses this depot. It's a big crop and the Yesil, Balkash and Kurgaldzhino districts are all sending their grain to us. Atbasar will have to receive and dispatch 50,000 tonnes at least."

"I see . . . " I turned to Simenkov. "Can we use this space for handling the grain?"

"In general terms it's possible," he replied. "But simply clearing the ground isn't enough. That would be a breach of regulations, and sheer negligence besides."

"What has to be done?"

"Plough it up, roll it, ram it. Disinfection is absolutely necessary. If we stick to the rules, you can count on ten days."

"Nikanor Georgievich, you've had a lot of experience. Isn't there any other way?"

"I've had to get round all kinds of corners in my time," Simenkov replied. "Sometimes you've got no choice. . . . We could burn the ground. Spread a lot of straw and give it a thorough scorching. That will calcinate the soil and it'll be as hard as an oven floor."

"What about disinfection?"

"The heat will do that."

"Then that's the way out of the situation!"

We were all silent for a while. We seemed to have considered everything. But then the head of the procurement depot stepped in.

"No, Leonid Ilyich, I don't agree. What difference does it make where the grain is? In the steppe it's out in the open and here with me it'll be out in the open too. The whole district couldn't provide a tarpaulin to cover piles of grain that size. It'll all be ruined!"

"We'll make sure you get all the rolling stock you need. I take that on myself."

"And what about that?" he pointed a thumb at the sky. "Will you take that on yourself too?"

It was a stiflingly hot autumn. The sun hardly moved, there wasn't a cloud in the sky, and the forecasts were encouraging. But who could guarantee against sudden rain?

"You know", Povliyanenko said, "that it is categorically forbidden to store grain in the open. I can't take on such a responsibility."

It would have been easy enough to reproach him for formalism and playing safe. But there was something about this grim-faced man that I liked. Some people would say "I'll fix it!" and then do nothing. (I shall have more to say later about one such person with an "I'll fix it!" for every occasion.) But Povliyanenko really would be receiving mountains of grain and he would be personally responsible for it. I could feel the anxiety among the other people as well: it's all

very well for you, they seemed to be saying, you give your instructions and off you go. But what about us? The weather's not under
our control, nor are the trains. And will we get them anyway?

"All right, let's sort this out," I said. "If we leave the grain out in
the fields, it'll be ruined for sure. They have no storehouses there
and when the roads are nothing but mud, and then the frosts come,
we'll never get it out. All that grain will be lost, we'll destroy all faith
in the virgin lands, and people will say we're just windbags, not
managers. And they'll be right. But here you have a road, a station,
rolling stock. There are thousands of people here who will help save
the grain in an emergency. We'll bring the troops in if necessary,
students, workers—they'll get out their shovels and load it, they'll
help. Can't you see the difference, Ivan Grigorievich? Where is it
safer for the grain—in the steppe or in the town?"

"Yes, everyone will help," Povilyanenko said. "But I'll be the one
who'll be up before the judge."

It was obvious that he didn't believe my promise of help. I didn't
want to offend him, but I had to get at his self-esteem.

"In the old days they used to say: what a man is like at war, so he'll
be like on the threshing floor. You didn't lose your grip at the front.
Why should you here? There are emergencies even in peacetime,
moments when we have to shout: "Watch out!" Besides, we could
well ask you: didn't you know before this that there was going to be a
bumper crop from the virgin lands? Why didn't you prepare for it
six months ago? Why didn't you do everything in your power? Well,
all right, we'll admit that we're at fault too. We'll share the blame,
half and half. But we'll hold you responsible for this patch of
ground, and strictly responsible! You've got to see to it that every
scrap of grain leaves here for the elevators, where it can be processed
and stored. We shall all answer together for this priceless grain."

The discussion ended with mutual undertakings. Ivan
Grigorievich, in the same gloomy way and without any grand promises, said that he would do everything he could. I felt he could be
trusted. To be quite honest, this man's stubborn obstinacy had

brought home to me, and indeed to all of us, the full importance of
the step we were taking. It had made us think twice, weigh all the
factors. And I, in my turn, promised not to let this station out of my
field of view.

Some people might say that this is not the kind of thing for a
secretary of the Central Committee of such a huge republic to be doing, that it's on too small a scale. Some of my fellow Party workers
thought it was hardly right for me to go into all these details myself,
even to the point of peering into the field workers' cooking pots.
Didn't this reduce the sense of responsibility of the lower-level officials? My reply to this is that no amount of paperwork, no number
of telephone calls are a substitute for meeting people and knowing
life. Unfortunately I have often seen for myself that all kinds of
reports, while travelling up through the departments, tend to get
distorted. And always in the one direction—towards toning down
the awkward facts.

Leadership from the office is not enough. One must be constantly
in touch with the people, go out and see with one's own eyes both the
successes and the difficulties and, if necessary, intervene. After an
argument with the people at a steppeland station, or after sitting
round the common pot with a team of tractor drivers, you come to
understand a lot and learn a lot. It is always a good thing to learn
something new, and when such major operations as the opening up
of the virgin lands are only just getting under way it is absolutely
essential.

What is more, such occurrences as the one I have just described
do not remain episodes of merely local significance. Not infrequent-
ly they result in major decisions. On returning to Alma-Ata I put the
matter of grain procurement before the Central Committee Buro
and a decision was taken on the matter. I got in touch with N. A.
Gundobin, Deputy Minister for Railways of the USSR, and told him
how urgent the problem was. In those days he spent nearly all his
time in the virgin lands, virtually taking charge of the main control
centre in Tselinograd. Day and night he kept a check on the move-

ment of freight and turn-round of traffic and was quick enough in responding to our requests. So the ripples from the "minor" episode spread out in circles, as it were, right across the virgin lands.

But let me return to the episode in Atbasar. The heat that year was utterly exhausting. After the talk at the procurement depot someone suggested going down to the river for a dip. But even there, of course, the talk was still about business.

I said to the leaders of the district, "Despite the great difficulties you face, your district can still do well in terms of grain deliveries. You can do it."

I did keep a close check on how things were going at Atbasar depot. I had to ask the republic's Minister for Procurement to go there urgently to provide practical help. I telephoned frequently to ask how much grain they had received, how much had been dispatched and what help was needed. All the precious grain was safely gathered in and later, when the Atbasar people had fulfilled their obligations (they had become initiators of a movement for above-plan deliveries), and when *Pravda* published a long article about their initiative — a good, useful initiative — I must confess that I felt a deep personal involvement in the success of the machine operators, the district Party committee people, purchasers and railwaymen. It had a deep effect on me.

In 1954, for the first time in its history, Kazakhstan poured four million tonnes of grain into our country's granaries — two-and-a-half million more than in the best years before that. All of us virgin landers felt the true happiness of that victory.

7.

After the autumn of 1954 the advance into the virgin lands developed on an even greater scale. In addition to the ninety new state farms already established, about 250 more had to be set up. The increase in the number of farms meant an equivalent increase in our commitments.

However, by this time the republic's Party organisation had gained experience in handling the day-to-day affairs of the virgin lands and a fairly clear-cut long-term programme of action was emerging. Many features of Kazakhstan's present-day agriculture, its structure and basic trends, were determined and began to take visible shape at that time, nearly a quarter of a century ago.

The things that particularly worried us in those days, the questions which were given priority, how the campaign for achieving our goals proceeded is partly described in my book *Questions of CPSU Agrarian Policy and the Opening Up of the Virgin Lands of Kazakhstan*. To avoid repetition I will give only the major policies, the long-term targets of those years:

by opening up the virgin and abandoned lands, and also by raising the yield on the old arable land, to make grain the main form of agriculture in Kazakhstan, to increase the production of grain there compared with the previous period not less than tenfold and thus turn the republic into a new major grain-producing area;

to evolve and gradually introduce in the virgin lands the scientific system of crop farming best suited for the extremely difficult climatic conditions and preserving and multiplying the natural fertility of the soil;

in setting up the country's largest grain-growing state farms to build for each of them everything they needed — both well-equipped

Early settlement houses in winter.

Ready for its first harvest: an early grain elevator.

Processing grain on a state farm.

"Too early to rest on our laurels": The Urneksky State Grain Farm wins an all-USSR prize
for its achievements, 1955.

A "first furrow".

Two decades later: A cereal production-complex, Kustanai region, 1978.

A school at the Lomonosov State Farm, Kustanai region, 1978.

production premises and comfortable urban-type housing with all the normal social and cultural services and public utilities. To completely reorganise, expand and remodel on the pattern of the new farms all the old state and collective farms of the republic;

in the shortest possible time to link up the virgin land regions by means of a network of railways, highways and inter-farm roads, to install power lines, telegraph, telephone and radio communications, to build at key points large-capacity elevators, factories for producing and repairing agricultural machinery, and dozens of other enterprises, and thus turn Northern Kazakhstan into a highly developed economic area, functioning as an integrated economic organism;

on the basis of increased grain production and by using its waste materials, and by means of a sharp expansion of the area under fodder crops, particularly maize, and also by raising the yields of the grasses sown and by improving the hayfields, to radically strengthen the fodder base and ensure a rapid growth of livestock breeding. In the long term to at least double all types of animal products;

in the south of the republic, by means of soil improvement, to intensively develop the cultivation of rice, cotton, beets, vegetables, fruit and grapes.

This programme was not an easy one. It also had to be carried out not bit by bit, but all at once. And, of course, one had to reckon with all the difficulties of the time and those that still lay in the future. So it was very important to inspire with faith and energy everyone with whom our work brought us into contact.

Take animal breeding. Quite a lot of our top officials let the campaign for grain eclipse everything else and neglected other important branches of agriculture.

Nevertheless we resolutely set about reorganising animal breeding. There were times when I was reproached for repeating some things too often. It's clear enough already, people would say, why keep on talking about the same thing? It was clear all right, but progress was slow and sometimes things did not move at all. It took a great deal of effort, for example, to develop maize, a crop that was virtually new to Kazakhstan. We intended ultimately to grow it for its grain as well, but for the time being most of the sowing was for silage. This aroused a kind of tacit resistance among local officials. Why would anyone want to raise "grass" on good ploughland? Again and again one had to argue, urge, show by example how to sow maize, cultivate it, harvest it and store it.

I knew the value of this crop from my experience in the Ukraine and Moldavia, but since I was no agronomist I decided to get an expert opinion. I wrote to M. E. Ozerny, the "maize magician", who was a friend of mine and lived in the village of Mishurin Rog in Dnepropetrovsk Region. Soon an answer arrived with some very valuable advice. At my request he also sent me varieties of seed suitable for the drylands of Kazakhstan. Things started to move, but still we had to put the matter before the Central Committee Buro and hold seminars on maize more than once.

The trial sowings made in the first spring had gone well and in 1955 we planted 700,000 hectares with this crop. Animal breeding also began to make headway, though not very quickly. It was perseverance that helped us in this, as in other matters. At a meeting of the republic's activists in March 1955 I said:

"There are some questions that one has to return to over and over again. What does this indicate? I think, on the one hand, the essential importance of the assignment and, on the other, the great difficulty in accomplishing it. Our persistence in raising these problems is yet another proof of the seriousness of our intentions. In order to push through our ideas we shall go on hammering away at the same spot without wavering or hesitation. The time is bound to come when these problems can be taken off the agenda. And then — of this we are also well aware — new questions, new tasks of even greater range and scope will arise."

Some of our officials could not grasp this. It seemed to them that the final goal had been achieved with the first harvest from the virgin lands. They sensed the possibility of a breather, and started reshuffling their personnel and recommending some for promotion. I don't mean that the people in question hadn't deserved it. On the contrary, I remember and deeply respect the first virgin land farm directors. They shouldered a massive burden and many of them later developed into high-powered managers. But at that moment it was too early to take people away from their posts.

One day I was approached by one of them, Fedor Trofimovich Morgun. He came to me with a complaint that could hardly be described as ordinary. He had been offered a higher position, but he didn't want it and was doing all he could to get out of it. There is no need for me to describe this man in detail because he later said it all himself in a book, *Thoughts on the Virgin Lands*. His state farm was one of the best and was often cited as an example to others, so now he had been recommended for the post of chairman of the district executive committee. What seemed to be an honour had upset him enormously. He had only just got the farm going, made friends with the people, worked out a plan for turning the farm into a veritable factory for producing cheap grain, and now he would have to abandon it all. I had to intervene personally, and this is what was said on the subject at a big conference:

"We cannot agree with the decision of the buro of the Kokchetav Regional Party Committee on the transfer of Comrade Morgun, director of the Tolbukhin State Farm, to other work, even though it entails promotion. There should be no hasty transferring of personnel. They must be helped to build up the state farms, master the system of cropping with an eye to the local soil and climatic conditions, allowed to complete the work they have begun, and only then be moved up to higher posts, if this should prove necessary."

Another example. Yevkdokia Andreevna Zaichukova was nearly fifty when she came to the virgin lands. But she had kept her youthful zest, willpower and strength of character and above all she had the ardent heart of a communist and patriot. She was moved to come to us by a deep and keenly felt desire to do everything that could and should be done for the country, and it was this that gave her the energy to set up the Dvurechny State Farm in the steppe. Soon she, too, was given a promotion. But after working for a while at her new post she wrote the following application:

"I firmly request the members of the district Party committee to release me from the post of first secretary of the district committee. I request this because I believe that the remaining years of my life could be spent with greater benefit to the Party and the people by working in a managerial capacity. I request to be sent to a backward state farm and promise that together with the Party members and all the workers there I will make it one of the leading farms of Tselinograd Region."

And she kept her word: under her directorship the Izhevsk State Farm did very well indeed. Yevdokia Andreevna gave seventeen years of her life to the new land that she had grown to love. And when she was dying, she asked the friends who came to see her in hospital only one thing:

"Don't put up any fences round my grave. Don't separate me from the steppe."

Such people are our greatest asset, the pride of the Party and the nation. And we treated them with special consideration. No one had the right to move the directors and managerial staff of the state farms, let alone dismiss them, without informing the Central Committee of the Kazakh Communist Party. As far as I remember we replaced not more than ten directors, and these were people for whom the burden of the virgin lands proved too heavy. The same policy applied to other officials. We actively supported the best, were patient and considerate with the promising, and resolutely removed those who obviously lacked ability or were lazy.

The bumper harvest focused general attention on the virgin lands, victory salutes were sounded in the press, it became customary to praise and congratulate us, but we knew that we could not afford to relax. It was too early to rest on our laurels. Kazakhstan's Party organisation was aware that we would have to push ahead with the construction of elevators and storage facilities

and get people out of the tents and dug-outs as soon as possible. This
was becoming an ever more complex and urgent problem.

Literally everything had to be built from scratch. But what with?
If there had been forests all round, the question would not have
arisen. Admittedly, the virgin lands were receiving prefabricated
houses and building materials, but not enough to go round. Our
plans ran ahead of our potential. Obviously, maximum use had to
be made of local resources. But by no means everyone was being as
efficient and resourceful as he could be.

Sometimes I would arrive at a district centre and ask how the construction work was going. Badly, they would say. Why? No bricks.
But then we would walk down the street with the Party district committee secretary and see solid brick buildings with dates on
them—1904, 1912. . . . And yet I knew for a fact that there were no
brickyards in this district and never had been.

"Who put up these buildings?"

"The *zemstvo*."*

"Where did they get the bricks?"

"Down there in the ravine. They built a scove kiln and fired them.
That's what this school is built of too."

"So the *zemstvo* could organise everything and you, the district
Party committee and the district executive committee can't? What
kind of leaders are we? There's plenty of clay all round, make some
scove kilns and set up a few brickyards. You can use them for
another hundred years."

"A brickyard? That's too big an undertaking for us."

It makes you angry to see people so passive!

In Barvikha, near Moscow, I happened to notice a splendid castle
built of brick. It was a holiday camp for Young Pioneers. I asked
about the building and was told that it used to be part of the estate
of some baroness or other. How had the castle been built? Quite
simply. The rich lady had ordered a brickyard to be set up, built

*zemstvo the local council of pre-revolutionary Russia.

herself this country residence and all its outbuildings with the bricks, then sold the brickyard and completely recovered all the costs of construction. Of course, she did not devise the whole scheme herself, she had had a sensible manager. Still, that's how it was done. But today we have whole production teams, experienced leaders, engineers, builders who set out on grandiose undertakings but cannot build an ordinary brickyard. Instead they rely on the state and apply to the State Planning Committee.

I recall how in the virgin lands we had to borrow the solid stable buildings constructed out of those same scove bricks from some of the old stud farms. We needed them for the repair shops on tractor stations. When I told people about this, when I managed to get through to them and make them feel ashamed of themselves I would soon find sensible managers arranging their own brick production. Afterwards they would thank me for it and wonder why they hadn't thought of it before.

One of the local building materials was rushes. On learning that a few enterprising people had already built themselves solid houses out of compressed rush slabs, I drove out to have a look and was quite satisfied with this form of housing. It would serve well enough for the first few years. This meant that we would have to gather rushes on a big scale and get the slabs into production. I consulted a map of the republic that showed the places where rushes grew and decided to see them in their natural state. I flew along the valley of the River Ili as far as Lake Balkhash. From an altitude of 100 metres it looked like a solid jungle of rushes!

Soon we organised the harvesting of rushes wherever they grew in any abundance — along the banks of rivers, around many steppeland lakes. Factories quickly manufactured simple, convenient and highly efficient machines that crushed and pressed them into solid slabs. These slabs were good for assembling buildings of any shape. When plastered and whitewashed they made splendid warm houses. After testing the process, we held a republic-wide seminar on rush-slab construction at a collective farm near Alma-Ata.

The republican Central Committee gave high priority to construction problems. The files still contain our memorandum to the CPSU Central Committee on what resources the republic had at its disposal when it set out to develop the virgin lands. Our forces were scattered; more than thirty low-capacity construction organisations were subordinated to various ministries and departments. All told they had 59 concrete mixers, 6 tower cranes, 58 conveyors, 5 motor hoists, and only 5,700 workers. To complete the new plans we needed at least ten times that number of people!

Construction materials, particularly bricks, were, of course, a big problem. I appealed to the leaders of a number of our republics and I must say that they were most helpful. Bricks started arriving from Armenia, Georgia, Estonia and many other places. In short, we dealt with the problems as they arose and dealt with them successfully.

8.

The Kazakhstan Writers' Congress in the autumn of 1954 was a major event in the cultural life of the republic.

It was not the first time I had been involved in matters connected with a national culture. Back in Moldavia I had realised that if you go to live in another republic you should get to know the customs and traditions of its people, their history and art. As soon as I arrived in Alma-Ata I laid in a stock of books, started meeting Kazakh writers and artists, and going to the theatre as often as possible. I had long had a liking for poetry and I read a great deal of the verse of the Kazakh poets, particularly Abai, whose lyricism, folk wisdom and deep knowledge of life appealed to me. Abai taught the Kazakh people not to isolate themselves, not to stand still, but to enrich their culture with the achievements of the Russian and other peoples. This message is still relevant. Any national culture that becomes wrapped up in itself inevitably puts itself at a disadvantage and loses its universal features. Unfortunately this is not always appreciated.

Socialism has long since proved that the more intense is the growth of each national republic, the more apparent becomes the process of internationalisation. Kazakhstan is perhaps the most vivid example of this. The virgin lands made it without exaggeration a "planet of one hundred tongues". And Kazakh culture forged ahead, absorbing all that was best in the other national cultures. Is this bad or good? We communists reply: it's good, very good! This vital question of national traditions and originality should never be oversimplified, reduced merely to ethnography, to everyday customs and traditions: to *izbas**, the *khorovod*** and *kokoshnik* †in Russia; and to *yurts* ‡ and herds of horses in Kazakhstan.

We in the Central Committee tried to give constant help to artists and writers. Despite all the difficulties of the virgin lands campaign, it was this period that saw the birth of the Kazakh State Song and Dance Ensemble, the revived publication of the newspaper *Kazakh adebieti,* and large-scale preparations for the ten-day festival of Kazakh literature and art in Moscow. This did not come about without debate. Some people wanted to concentrate entirely on the oral art of the *akyns*‖. But fundamental changes were taking place in the literature of the republic. They stemmed from the progress being made in the building of socialism and the growth of the Kazakh intelligentsia. Gifted young people who knew and loved not only the old traditions and songs, but were well versed in Soviet and world literature, had come upon the scene. These were people with

---

*izba the traditional peasant cottage.
**khorovod a gliding Russian folk dance.
†*kokoshnik* woman's head-dress in old Russia.
‡*yurt* the felt tent of the steppe-dwellers.
‖*akyn* Kazakh bard.

free untrammeled minds and they had to be supported. But the main thing was to improve the atmosphere in the artistic unions, among the intellectuals. They had to be rallied, their forces had to be united to cope with the tremendous tasks facing the republic.

Incidentally I would like to note that champions of national exclusiveness masquerading as defenders of "the purity of the national tradition" usually act deviously and rarely come out into the open. On the contrary, they try to appear "holier than the pope" by cleverly exploiting any mistakes made by their opponents. I remember all the hue and cry over the role of a certain Kenesary. At first he was declared to have been a progressive figure favouring the union of Kazakhstan with Russia. Later, documents were found indicating that he was a reactionary and did not approve of the union. . . . I have no desire to dig up past history, and besides, I don't regard myself as a specialist in this area. What worried me was something else. The battles that certain demagogues provoked had made such outstanding people as the writer Mukhtar Auezov and Academician Kanysh Satpaev leave the republic.

We helped them return to Alma-Ata. That splendid scientist Kanysh Imantaevich Satpaev has given tremendous service in the development of Kazakhstan's productive forces. Mukhtar Omarkhanovich Auezov is an acknowledged master of Kazakh literature. It is with much gratitude that I recall these people, how we often met, how we worked closely together, and how much I simply enjoyed a very human friendship with them. In our talks we often spoke of the fact that all extremes are harmful. The oral art so much loved by the people, should not be forgotten. "Leningraders, my children!" — the whole country remembers those inspired lines of Dzhambul's. Let the art of the *akyns* live and develop in the general stream of Kazakh and Soviet literature.

At this time I had another problem on my mind: how to focus the attention of the writers and artists on the virgin lands theme! Just look at the things that are taking place before our very eyes, I said at a meeting with writers at the Central Committee. Huge masses of people are on the move, multi-national collectives are being formed, new families are being born, characters are maturing, the heroes of our time are being tested and toughened. In Kazakhstan bread was always a delicacy, something precious. Even the mullahs used to say in the old days, "The Koran is a sacred book but one can tread on the Koran if one needs to in order to reach a crumb of bread." And now this region is to have an abundance of bread. The whole structure of life is changing, people are acquiring a new attitude to life. Shouldn't the greatness, the dramatic appeal of what is happening stir the inspiration of the true artist? No one will understand us now or in the future if this epic is not vividly recorded for history.

In these circumstances it was important that the Congress of Writers of the republic should become a festival of Soviet literature as a whole. We invited Mikhail Sholokhov, Leonid Leonov, Kamil Yashen, Mirzo Tursun-zadeh, Maxim Tank and other famous writers to attend. After this composers, actors and artists became frequent visitors to the virgin lands, articles and stories about the battle for grain were published, motion pictures appeared, plays were produced and new songs were sung. They undoubtedly played a positive role.

It was my dream that one day the epic of the virgin lands would be reflected in works of art as profoundly and powerfully as the civil war is reflected in *And Quiet Flows the Don,* and collectivisation in *Virgin Soil Upturned.* For the writer and artist there is surely no more inspiring task than to portray the feats of the people, and this should include those performed in the virgin lands.

9.

The year 1955 was called the "year of desperation" in the new lands. My own assessment would not be so extreme, although things were very tough. All summer, from May onwards, not a single drop of rain fell. We waited in vain for the rains that come regularly in June. This meant that we had to be prepared for the worst.

Anyone who has not been in the steppe at such a time cannot understand the feelings of the grain grower. It is a strange sensation: in spring the steppe would sometimes be turned into a sea by flood-waters and people would have to reach their work-teams by boat. But as soon as the spring rains stopped, the water disappeared. From early morning the scorching sun would begin its work of destruction. It would drift slowly across the whitish faded sky, pouring down its intolerable sultry heat until evening, when the purple-red orb would sink in a turbid haze below the horizon. And the next day, almost without respite, it would rise again and go on burning the life out of everything. And this went on week after week, month after month.

Meanwhile we had doubled the crop area in comparison with the previous year. Nearly ten million hectares of grain had been planted on the newly cultivated land. One-and-a-half million hectares over and above the plan had been sown in spring. And the sowing had been carried out faster and better than in the previous season. In one year the republic had taken a huge step forward in crop farming. People could already see the results of their labours and continued to work with a will, not yet knowing the disaster that awaited them.

We knew, of course, that heat and drought were nothing out of the ordinary in this region. But we did not yet know the implacable perversity of the steppeland calendar, which once in ten years brings particularly cruel and destructive droughts upon the land. We foresaw, even before launching our offensive, that a battle with the elements was inevitable. When the economics of opening up the virgin lands were worked out, the experts estimated that even if there were two years of severe drought in every five we should still receive an average of eight million tonnes of grain per year. There was no reason to doubt these estimates. We knew what we were getting into, but it is one thing to know and quite another to see the precious harvest that has taken such effort to grow, perish before your eyes.

How people crave for rain at such a time! The nervous tension builds up beyond endurance. The merest rustle against a window-pane can bring people rushing out of their homes at night. "Rain!" But no, it is not raindrops pattering on the windows and roof, but dust driven by the dry wind.

In the steppe it is difficult to breathe. The air sears the lungs like the breath of a furnace. As at times of intense cold, the birds do not fly. Plants dry up, lose their leaves and wither into dust. The ground breaks up into deep cracks, big enough to swallow a crowbar. The huge masses of wheat turn grey, then white and the empty ears rustle where the grain did not have time to ripen. And then to crown everything, the hot storms come, lifting clouds of dust, tearing down telegraph lines and ripping off roofs.

One can understand the pain a farmer feels when he sees how relentlessly everything is being destroyed, all the fruit of his year's work, all his efforts and hopes. And one needs a sturdy spirit and strong nerves to stand this test. Even the knowledge that next season the steppes should redeem all that has been lost does not help very much; one always wants the harvest today, now.

I have no wish to oversimplify the situation, to make things appear better than they were. In those months we at the Central Committee began to receive letters from people asking what was to be done, how to carry on.

The republican Central Committee Buro decided to hold meetings in all the virgin land farm production teams and honestly describe the state of affairs, to try to put some heart into the people, direct their attention to the tasks that would take priority under such conditions, and explain that in crop farming each year differs from the next, and that the time would come when our virgin lands would have it good again. At the same time I warned those who went out to the farms not to act as if there was nothing to worry about. Such were the main objectives of Party work among the masses at that moment.

I must say that after the frank and open discussions that were held at every state farm the virgin landers got down to work with renewed zest. Despite the blazing sun we went on preparing for the harvest and were busy laying in stocks of animal feed right up to late autumn. We pushed ahead with construction even more widely and actively, particularly on the state farms. Food and manufactured goods were coming into the virgin lands in large enough quantities to guarantee uninterrupted supplies for the whole winter.

We found support and help at the CPSU Central Committee.

I must express my warmest gratitude to the members of the Politburo and the secretaries of the CPSU Central Committee, who did so much in those years to bring the virgin lands quickly and successfully under cultivation. I often met and consulted with them and always received precise, specific answers to my questions, firm Party backing and generous moral support.

Despite the difficulties we continued our work with confidence in 1955. What was the basis of this confidence? Certainly we were all bitterly disappointed that the tremendous effort we had put into the soil had not produced the desired results. A number of farms, however, had reaped a decent harvest. The Zhdanov State Farm, Kokchetav Region, set up in 1954, had brought in 7.9 centners per hectare from an area of 22,500 hectares, while the Roslavl State

Farm, Alma-Ata Region, yielded 9.1 centners from each of its 20,000 hectares. And farms like these were not so few in number. Whole districts and even regions, such as North Kazakhstan and Kokchetav, gathered harvests that were not at all bad for those days. We should have to make a thorough investigation into what had helped some to bring in their grain and what had left others with nothing but scorched fields. I must add that despite the low average yield the republic still received 80 per cent of its total grain harvest that year from the virgin lands. Kazakhstan again laid in considerably more coarse feed than before the virgin lands were opened up, and supplied 85,000 tons more milk and 122,000 tons more meat. Nearly one-and-a-half million tons of silage, mainly maize, were stored. These were, of course, modest successes, but they showed that the virgin lands were already playing and would continue to play an ever increasing role in boosting output of grain and other farm produce. So keep working! That was our watchword.

But a harvest failure is a harvest failure, and it made many problems much more difficult to solve.

At the end of 1955 I was in Moscow at a meeting of Party and government officials from throughout the Soviet Union. One feels uncomfortable, of course, at such gatherings, when people go on asking you endless questions or, conversely, express their sympathy by deliberately talking about something else. And when I declared from the conference platform that the following year Kazakhstan would supply the state with ten million tonnes of grain, an incredulous murmur broke out all over the hall.

How times have changed! If we tried nowadays to set a target of eight to ten million tonnes a year for the virgin lands, which then seemed a huge amount, it would be regarded as a serious defeat. Nowadays we receive on average about sixteen million tonnes of Kazakhstan grain per year!

In Japan, as I. A. Goncharov relates in *The Frigate 'Pallada'*, provincial governors in the old days used to answer with their heads for everything that happened — typhoons, cloudbursts and earthquakes.

Our heads did not seem to be in danger, but after the unfortunate course of events in 1955 one had an oppressive sense of being guilty of something for which one was not really to blame. I have not forgotten that feeling. And today I sometimes call up districts that have suffered natural disasters simply to offer a word of encouragement to the people in charge. On one occasion I was invited to Ulyanovsk Region: "Leonid Ilyich, come and have a look, we've got a wonderful crop of grain!" But then the dry winds began to blow and everything was burnt up. Understandably, the first secretary of the regional Party committee was embarrassed, upset and worried. I discussed things with him in the usual calm way. We had to agree upon what measures should be taken and how to help the local officials.

But during that year of disaster we, who all along were confident of success, sometimes had difficulty in proving that we were right. When at one of the big conferences I declared in the presence of Khrushchev that the virgin lands would show their true worth yet, he interrupted me rather sharply, "We can't make pies out of your promises!"

But I had every reason to answer him firmly, "All the same we believe that soon, very soon there will be a bumper grain crop in the virgin lands!"

We took great pains to prepare for the new spring. There was only one salvation, one hope, one remedy—work. In 1956, 27 million hectares of virgin land were to be sown, and 22 million of them to grain crops. And once again I wanted to see everything, meet everyone, get everything done in time. . . .

10.

To increase the production of grain, meat, and vegetables we now assign huge material and financial resources that were quite beyond our dreams in those years. We are introducing the latest machinery into agriculture; we always encourage the specialisation and concentration of production; and we are undertaking such integrated programmes as the transformation of the ancient Russian non-black-earth lands. These areas are our front line today.

But there is one thing we must never forget: for the national economy there is no "rear line". One still runs into people who are prepared to spend billions, but who lose sight of the so-called trifles. And yet one of the key tasks is to make careful and rational use of everything that we have at our disposal, everything that is produced in the country. Extravagance is impermissible; the more of the economy involved the more painful the effects of such mismanagement.

This was brought home to me while I was still in the virgin lands, so I do not want to lose sight of those "trifles" upon which so much in the life of the people depends. For instance, when I was on a big trip round Northern Kazakhstan, I arrived at the Izobilny State Farm, Tselinograd Region. It was situated far out in the steppe, on the River Selety, in a picturesque but at that time very wild spot. I had been there before, at the very beginning, and seen the first nine tents. This time I found a whole settlement. There were apartment houses, cafeteria, a shop, a bath-house, a bakery, workshops, a general office and a garage. In addition, and this was particularly important, people had built themselves nearly eighty private cottages. This meant that they really had settled in for good.

I got into conversation with them and began asking what they needed and how things were going. And this is what I heard.

"We're short of barrels. There's nothing to salt the cucumbers in."

"We want a pig, but where can we buy one?"

"It'll be good to have a calf. . . . "

These were not idle questions. A great deal of everything had been pumped into the virgin lands. Yet here we were with a shortage of barrels. And animals too. And not only as an addition to the larder. In our first year I had seen newcomers arriving, a suitcase in one hand and a basket with a pup or a cat in the other. A lad from Zaporozhe turned up at the Yaroslavl State Farm with a live rooster in a cage. "The best alarm-clock for the steppe," he told me. A joke, of course, but on that bare earth the rooster was a joy to everyone. The lads even managed to tame marmots and some of the steppeland birds.

One could regard all this as mere whimsy. But life has taught me to understand such things and treat them with respect. In my childhood I, myself, loved to watch a flight of pigeons on the wing. Of course, the main thing for us in the virgin lands was the millions of hectares and tonnes of grain, but people had to be helped to start up their personal vegetable gardens, to raise animals and poultry. Without that we would not have the hectares or the grain. The countryman with no livestock and plot of land in his keeping is like a tree without roots. In those years it was important for us to show from the first that we intended to make the steppe really habitable, and have it that way forever.

While pondering on this subject I looked across the fields and suddenly noticed yet another newcomer: a lonely rook was strutting across the black ploughland like a fault-finding agronomist. And the rook, as we all know, is a field bird. If it had flown all the way here, it must have come to stay.

I remembered the talk at Izobilny Farm and later turned up some old documents. Back in 1934 a Central Committee memorandum had been sent to the Kazakhstan Territory Party Committee. It had posed very broadly and firmly the question of developing horticulture both in rural areas and in the industrial districts. Thorough to the last detail, the memorandum proposed that this sphere should be given the most active and thorough assistance by Party and government bodies and also the leaders of collective and state farms and co-operatives. And horticulture soon developed a reliable material base. But years passed and suddenly it started to decline, shrinking to almost half its former size. And yet the republic had been receiving two-and-a-half times as many potatoes, for instance, from the personal vegetable patches as it had from the collective and state farms.

When one criticised certain directors for feeding their people on noodles and skilly the reply was always the same: we're short of supplies, give us supplies! There is no denying that some products should be centrally allocated to the rural areas, but why should they require allocations for potatoes, cabbage, cucumbers and watermelons? All these can be grown on any farm. The same applies to eggs and milk. From time immemorial the peasant has kept chickens and sold eggs in town. Why should he now receive every egg on a warrant from Moscow?

What I am writing about is still highly relevant today. There are still a good many officials who do nothing but rely on the almighty allocation without giving a second thought to where the state is to find the products they demand. In our country we must use every opportunity and every scrap of land to increase the output of farm products, to have "a bit extra" for our common table. Sometimes from a train window one sees patches of cluttered wasteground that could easily be used for cultivation, sowing grass, keeping animals. All this would mean more and better supplies from local resources, instead of having to bring, say, tomatoes and cucumbers all the way from the south, and eggs, cottage cheese and milk from places hundreds of kilometres away.

These things must be kept in mind by Party, government and economic bodies, and by the leaders of industry. It is their duty to develop solid agricultural bases around both large and small towns, to build up specialised complexes and subsidiary units, so as to ensure that there are plenty of potatoes, meat, milk, green vegetables and fruit in the shops. This can be done in Sverdlovsk, in Tyumen, in Irkutsk, or in any other city of the USSR. This was something I again had to point out to local officials during a trip round the Urals, Siberia and the Far East in the spring of 1978.

But in Kazakhstan, way back in 1955, a decision was taken to develop private-sector vegetable-growing on a broad scale, to give everyone who wanted it a plot of land, make implements available and give every possible assistance. The same policy was adopted for poultry and the sale of animals for personal use. It was no less important to organise subsidiary units in all the state farms. Here a strange situation had arisen. By the time the virgin lands project was launched the number of such units had dwindled to almost a quarter of their peak level. In the midst of their global plans and grandiose projects some people had abandoned what seemed to them of secondary importance.

These "trifles" — and figures will be of some use here — presented the following picture: the number of cows in subsidiary holdings had fallen by 11,000, sheep by 280,000; 3,700 hectares of gourd crops, 5,000 hectares of vegetables and 11,000 hectares of potatoes had disappeared, no one knew where. The country was still living under difficult conditions and yet here we were being deprived of a huge amount of produce. Urgent measures had to be taken. Funds and land were allocated for subsidiary units, dairy animals were brought in, hot-houses and poultry sheds were built, soft-fruit plantations laid out; their production was written into the plans of the state farms and the directors were held strictly responsible for fulfilment. All this was important both for improving supplies for the virgin landers and to give people the psychological lift of seeing that life in the steppe was getting better.

Recalling all this and reading the documents from those years, I noticed how often I mentioned Kurgaldzhino District. In those days I was very upset over its affairs, and particularly by what I saw during one of my visits to the Stepnyak State Farm. I visited this farm for the first time in the summer of 1954 and was confronted with a sad picture. In some places you feel immediately that something is wrong. Crowds of people attach themselves to any newcomer and follow him about complaining. I, too, was immediately buttonholed by a woman, who poured out her story.

"Comrade representative, I don't know who you are, but take an interest, help us. We haven't any electricity, any fuel, any kerosene even. There's nothing to cook with. And there's nothing to cook either. . . . "

I went into the local shop with her. There was not even any salt. Another woman, with a child, addressed me no less anxiously.

"Comrade Brezhnev, there's no milk, no semolina. Tell us what we're supposed to feed the children on. You must have children yourself. You're a father, so help us."

I asked to see the representative of the workers' co-operative. Without batting an eyelid he declared that semolina had been out of stock for only one day. But his shifty eyes told me he was lying. I promised the women I would investigate the shortage of groceries, but what surprised me even more was the lack of milk. By then we had given many state farms, including the Stepnyak, animals for the workers who wanted to keep them as a source of food products for the farms' own consumption. We had asked for a report on how many cows, pigs, horses and poultry had been allotted and to whom, and had let the matter rest there. But while I was walking round the farm, the crowd steered me into the cafeteria and we sat down to talk things over.

"How many cows have you got?"

"About fifty."

"Then you ought to have enough milk."

"Some hope! They're sixty kilometres from here. They're out for pasturing."

By this time they had found the director, Kovalenko. He hurried in and started complaining at once.

"It's terrible, Leonid Ilyich! I can't persuade any of the women to work in the dairy. None of them want to milk the cows."

"So they're not being milked while they're at pasture?"

"That's right."

"Aren't you worried about the children going without milk and the harm being done to the cows?"

"Worried? I'm terrified. I wouldn't be surprised if I end up in front of the judge. But don't worry, I'll fix it. . . . I've already sent a letter to the Ukraine. I'm inviting some girls to come and help us out."

I obviously wasn't going to get any more out of him, and so I turned to the women.

"Why don't you help? You can see what the situation is."

"What can we do with the children?" they burst out. "We've all got families, children."

"Suppose we give each of you a cow for a while, then will you look after them and milk them?"

"Of course we will! We'll milk them and drive them out into the steppe. And our husbands can milk them too."

"Well, Comrade Kovalenko, there you are, ready to go to gaol and you couldn't even think of a simple thing like that? Distribute the cows among the workers. They can milk them and feed their children. And later on you can get your full-time people."

"I never thought of that. I'll fix it. . . . "

I went round the settlement with the director. I could see that the construction work was being done badly. The houses were jerry-built, without any proper foundations. I gave him a piece of my mind. To be quite honest, I had already begun to distrust Kovalenko because of his perpetual repetition of the phrase: "I'll fix it. . . . " I impressed upon him that I would come back and check up on everything. But the next time I visited the Stepnyak Farm I was astounded to find that almost nothing had changed! Supplies in the shop and the cafeteria were better, but that was because of the previous year's intervention. In other matters Kovalenko himself had not lifted a finger. The people were still having problems, even with water, although on my last visit I had told the director to put a water-tank on a truck and have it deliver water to the houses — not much of a problem, it seemed to me. But once again in reply to everything I said, I got the same old reply, "I'll fix it. . . . "

Inefficiency there was, but examples of such staggering helplessness and indifference were rare on the virgin lands. Officials who neglected their duties so disgracefully could not be tolerated and I had to point this out at the next plenary meeting of the Tselinograd Regional Party Committee. Provision of amenities means providing for people, taking their needs into consideration. It is more than a purely economic task. Above all, it involves policy, and mistakes in this area are costly. For our mistakes we always pay heavily: at war we pay in lives; during peacetime, in physical and emotional resources.

To ensure a proper and full life in the area, the settlements in the steppe had to be in the charge of people who were not merely concerned with fulfilling the plan, but who felt a responsibility for everything that goes to make up people's lives. In Kokchetav Region, for instance, I liked visiting the "Red Army" Collective Farm. Not simply because it was well managed, but because they baked such wonderfully tasty bread. I don't think I have eaten better bread anywhere. It was so full-bodied and fragrant. It was particularly good in Petr Ivanovich Nikolaev's team. "When we're baking", he would say, "you can smell it a mile away!" I remember I once asked for a few loaves as a special treat for my colleagues in Alma-Ata and to teach the city's bakers how the job should be done.

While visiting the settlements I would rejoice over every properly made well, every carefully planted sapling. I was delighted by the

Young settlers of today.

Galya Gulyaeva, tractor driver. She works at the Lomonosov State Farm and was allocated tractor K-701 by the local branch of the Young Communist League in 1978. Her example has been followed by other girls.

S. V. Kalchenko, one of the first virgin landers, at a meeting with leading
agriculturalists from Kazakhstan, 1978.

"Things that are both heartening and impressive": The Lomonosov State Farm team receives the Red Banner award from the Borovsky *raikom*, Kustanai region, 1978, for the best grain harvest in the district.

The traditional Russian greeting of "bread and salt": Brezhnev arriving at Alma-Ata on a recent re-visit.

care that some people put into growing flowers and trees, and amaz-
ed at the indifference with which others treated the appearance of
their house, garden and settlement as a whole.

I once spent the night in a village in the former Galkin District in
Pavlodar Region (unfortunately, I have forgotten the name of the
village and the collective farm chairman with whom I stayed). In
the morning I went out for a walk through the village and was rather
surprised. It only had two streets, but along one there were trees in
front of some of the houses, while the other was completely bare.
What was the reason? The chairman told me the following story.

The village had once been visited by the governor of the Steppe
Territory, based in the city of Omsk. Before the revolution the present Northern Kazakhstan steppes formed part of his territory. During his visit the governor ordered every family to plant as many trees
in front of their houses as there were members in the family. Three
years later he revisited the village to see whether his order had been
obeyed. He found that some houses had trees in front of them while
others were in the same bare and dusty state as before. He then
ordered all the people living in the village — in those days it only had
one street — to come out with their families and stand at the gates of
their houses. He handed a soldier a belt with a heavy buckle and
walked down the street. To the householders who had planted trees
he said thank you and gave a silver ruble. But those who had
neglected his command he ordered to be thrashed with the
belt — one stroke for every missing tree. And while the punishment
was being administered the governor would shout, "Use the buckle,
Vasily, use the buckle!"

"And that was how the trees appeared in the streets," the chairman concluded with a laugh.

Joking apart, one had to campaign very hard to get trees planted
on the new state farms even in our day. And now, when I come to
the virgin lands and see the settlements buried in greenery, the rustl-
ing shady parks, the blossoming apple and cherry trees, the locust-
trees and lilac, the tempting gleam of innumerable ponds and reser-

voirs with the inevitable anglers on the sun-scorched banks—I recall
with a smile the story of the governor from Omsk.

11.

I had to travel a lot, sometimes by train, more often by air, and
sometimes in the course of one trip both. This combination saved a
good deal of time, which was always in short supply. During long
stops at junctions or regional centres, the train carriage served as a
hotel. A plane would be waiting for me and in the course of a day I
would be able to make flying visits to several districts or state farms.

An AN-2 had been specially fitted out for me in Kiev. It carried a
powerful radio-transmitter and there were six seats in the passenger
compartment. The crew also carried a folding bed, which was kept
in the tail. In all other respects it was the same reliable AN-2
workhorse that everyone knows so well. For our travels it was indispensable. The pilots knew how to choose a landing strip from the
air and in the steppe they could land anywhere, any furrow, tractor
or camp in the fields.

Convenient though it was, this air-taxi service did wear you out. I
had got used to it somehow, but one day our popular film-stars
Lyubov Orlova, Marina Ladynina and Nikolai Kryucnkov had to go
through it. They had come to entertain the virgin landers, but there
was no audience: everyone was far away in the steppe. "We did a
show in Kustanai," they complained to me, "but we want to see the
virgin landers themselves. Can't you help us with some transport?"

"Well, why not? Here's my plane," I replied, and told the pilots,
"Tomorrow I shall be busy in town and you will take these visitors
round the work-teams. Wherever you see people, go in and land."

The pilots did their best. In one day they flew round two or even three districts. It was a windy day, the turbulence was bad, and the actors came back to town feeling more dead than alive. Kryuchkov—a tough character—was still firm on his feet, but the women were worn out. I looked at them and reproached the pilot.

"It looks as if you've overdone it, Nikolai."

"But they insisted. When they got out of the plane, they would lie down for a bit under the wing, then give their show, and then it was 'Take us somewhere else.' Very brave women. . . . "

I thanked the actors but noticed that they no longer eyed my plane with the same envy as in the morning.

There were some days when we had to spend hours circling over the steppe. One day the pilot said to me: "I think we can put you down as a pilot. You've got a hundred hours up."

"What's the quota for pilots?"

"A hundred and twenty."

"Then it's too early for me to be a pilot."

"That depends. We're not doing normal flying."

"Isn't this normal?"

"What's our working altitude? A hundred metres. And how much hedgehopping do we have to do to find a landing strip? You can count every hour as two in these conditions."

I liked the crew—the captain Nikolai Moiseev, second pilot Mubin Abishev, and flight engineer Alexander Kruglikov. Their little plane, the "mosquito", as they called it, had been through any number of adventures. In the steppe, where there are no more than fifty windless days in the year, the little plane was always tossed about furiously. And even on the ground it got no peace: on a good many occasions loaded dump-trucks had to be brought up to anchor the plane so that it would not be overturned and smashed by the wind. It had to fly all the year round, regardless of the weather and sometimes breaking regulations. We landed after sunset and even at night, which is categorically forbidden in the AN-2. But our business didn't fit in with the regulations. My constant travelling companions, I realised, were past masters in their profession.

In those days many airmen dreamed of high speeds and long-distance flights in jet planes, and my pilots probably had similar thoughts. But they didn't let it worry them. They had their duties and they patiently and honestly carried them out. Only once did I see them very worried, almost scared. It happened, if I am not mistaken, at the Taman Division State Farm. We flew out to a work-team at the far end of the farm. It was May and the grass was already a lush green. The weather was clear and beneath us the steppe lay flat as a pancake. There was no problem finding a place to land. We landed, so it seemed to me, without any trouble. But as soon as the engine stopped, the first pilot, who usually left the plane after me, literally ran for the exit with an abrupt "Excuse me. . . . "

I followed him out and saw him hurrying along the tracks left in the grass by our wheels. He was looking for something. Eventually he stopped, waved his arms and started shouting to the tractor drivers who were working nearby. A crowd gathered. I joined them and Moiseev, pale and angry, said, "Look!"

In the grass half a metre away from the track of our left wheel lay a harrow, its teeth pointing skywards. From the air no one could have seen it and Moiseev had noticed it only as the plane touched down. There could have been a nasty accident. I could hardly restrain the airmen, who were about to have a punch-up with the team-leader and the tractor drivers. Of course, they could not possibly have known that a plane was going to land on that particular field, but the harrow, like anything else once you have finished with it, should have been put away and not just left lying around. It was an incident which clearly showed that bad management and carelessness are always on the borderline of becoming criminal negligence.

When I was leaving Kazakhstan and we said goodbye, the captain of the plane told me that in two years he had made 480 landings with me in various parts of the steppe. He said it with pride and I could understand his feelings as a professional. Knowing the skill of this splendid pilot, when I came to the virgin lands later as a secretary of the CPSU Central Committee, I flew only with Nikolai Grigorievich Moiseev.

So once again our project was in full swing, I was on the road all the time, slept in snatches, ate what was going. And one day in Tselinograd I suddenly felt ill. When I came to, I was lying on a stretcher. Once before I had been taken from Semipalatinsk to Alma-Ata with a heart attack. I had to rest at home, fending off the doctors, who kept trying to get me into hospital. I used to joke my way out of it: once you get hold of me, you'll keep me for good. But the real point was that I had no time to be ill. The virgin lands were always providing new projects and problems — difficult, sometimes muddled and always urgent.

The battle for grain had entered its decisive stage.

12.

I should like to deal briefly with our agricultural policy in the virgin lands. Weren't there any mistakes at all in our work? No, I cannot say that. Didn't we know that we were venturing into a particularly hazardous area for farming? Yes, we did, and we were prepared for it. Hadn't we heard the warnings of the experts that large-scale ploughing could turn the steppes into a desert? Of course we had, and had taken them into account. The Party's agricultural policy in the virgin lands, to put it briefly, was to reduce to the minimum the negative effects of human intervention in the primeval nature of the steppe, to establish the best field cropping practices, and then to evolve a system of crop farming well adapted to this drought-threatened area. But what this policy would be in specific terms, we did not know at first and could not have known.

There is an oriental proverb that says, "He who keeps walking will go all the way." Some time before the revolution Lenin wrote:

"The Russian working class will win their freedom and give an impetus to Europe by their revolutionary action, full though it be of errors — and let the philistines pride themselves on the infallibility of their revolutionary inaction."

Infallibility of inaction — an apt phrase! It would have been the easiest thing in the world to have left nature's larder untouched. That would have ruled out any possibility of error. But we came to these ancient steppes with a profound belief in the power of human reason. We were convinced that in the course of our work on this huge project, which was of such importance to the nation, we should find a means of preserving the fertility of the soil. And we searched for this new means from the outset.

We were fairly quick in abolishing pre-seedtime spring ploughing. On the whole we had only May, June and autumn-ploughed fallow, we introduced the planting of windbreak rows, organised snow retention, made sure we had a reliable fallow area. In short, we did everything we could to solve the main problem in farming a drought-threatened steppeland zone — retaining the moisture in the soil. We also sorted out the sowing schedule, although this was by no means a simple problem. Today no one in the virgin lands sows before the second half of May. This is now regarded as elementary. But in those days. . . . "Sow in mud and you'll be a lord!" was the old saying that people repeated everywhere. And some experts also insisted on early sowing in the virgin lands.

There were, however, other points of view, and the experience of even the first year showed that the fields sown in May yielded a splendid crop. What was the reason — the fresh vigour of the virgin soil or the late sowing? In 1955 late sowings were far more numerous and they obviously stood up better to the drought. This seemed to clinch matters, but the debate continued. It was particularly hard to convince the old-timers. At the "Red Army" Collective Farm, team leader Nikolaev, who had treated me to such tasty bread, ended our discussion of the matter on the following note:

"We'll try, of course, but you can't imagine how hard it will be to hold the men back. As soon as they see they can get a harrow on the fields, they start sowing—fast! That's what they're used to."

All the same, by the spring of 1956, in many of the new farms early sowing was regarded as something quite out of the ordinary, just as late sowing had been before. But old habits die hard. The first secretary of the Yesil District Party Committee, Anatoly Rodionovich Nikulin, a splendid organiser who became a Hero of Socialist Labour in the virgin lands, once told me in Moscow how one of the directors in his district insisted on ignoring the new sowing schedule.

"This fellow really distinguished himself. We hadn't even celebrated May Day and suddenly in marches this "champion": "Comrade Secretary, the farm has finished sowing!" Then he salutes and clicks his heels. I nearly jumped out of my chair: "You idiot! Why the hurry?" Because he wanted to be first in the district, he says. "Well, you'll have no grain to show for it!" I told him.

And he didn't. The district harvested 16 centners per hectare on average, while the "pace-setter" produced only six. It all happened a long time ago and after that incident the director had a fine record, which is why I don't mention his name. But how hard it is to stop people wanting to be the first to report the job done, but without even thinking whether anything will grow there afterwards.

But that is not the worst that can happen. Sometimes they do the ploughing well and sow according to schedule, but then, during harvesting, transportation, storage and processing lose nearly a third of the yield. Reducing waste is an area where so much can be done in farming today. Surely it is obvious that far less energy and funds are required to preserve what has been produced than to produce it. So attacking this problem has considerable advantages. It corresponds to the Party's policy of raising efficiency, and, above all, it serves the interests of the people.

I have a special respect for people in agriculture who calmly get on with the job, without a lot of fuss or noise and always keeping the ultimate goal in sight. There were quite a few farming practices that had to be rethought for the virgin lands. For instance, it was just as important for us to know how deep to sow as when to sow. It was no accident, as it turned out, that Kokchetav Region stood up to the 1955 drought better than others. During a visit to the Zhdanov State Farm at sowing time I noticed that the seeds were being planted unusually deep. M. G. Roginets, the regional Party secretary, described "just one little thing", not for the first time, if you remember the problems with the depth of the furrow in Chapter Three!

"Our agronomist maintains that the seeds should be planted at a depth of six or even eight centimetres, not at three or four centimetres as the virgin land regulations require."

"But they only sow maize that deep."

Unfortunately I don't remember the name of that agronomist, but I remember his explanation.

"You see, Leonid Ilyich, I had experimental plots with plantings at that depth last year. There's no comparison! The secret is simple: the upper layer of soil dries out quickly in these parts and before the plant can put down roots the ground cracks and tears them apart. With our method the roots have a chance to develop properly and draw up the lower moisture, and by that time the rains have come along to help them."

For two days I watched the new method of sowing. From the Zhdanov Farm that agronomist and I flew to the Chernigov Farm, then to other state farms. We readjusted the seed drills, crawled along the furrows and wore our fingers out poking the soil to test how deep the seeds were planted. But it was a fact that when the dry wind blew the plantings on these farms stayed greener the longest — green islands amid the brown sun-scorched steppe. So it was a worthwhile idea. Now in the virgin lands it has become the accepted procedure to plant to a depth of eight centimetres.

So we gleaned experience, grain by grain. But fresh troubles followed in the wake of success. The predictions of the experts about wind erosion began to come true. I remember how in Pavlodar Region together with district Party secretaries D. A. Asanov and I. F. Kaburneev I saw the first tornadoes moving across the fields and the sand banking up on the roads. It was a real "black storm" and you could hardly breathe. And soon after that the weeds appeared.

All this prompted me to go to Kurgan Region, to see T. S. Maltsev at the "Lenin's Legacy" Collective Farm. Terenty Semenovich showed me some clean plantings of wheat without a single weed among them, then gave me his view of the problem. This man has a deep sense of conviction that comes from years of experience, folk wisdom and devotion to the soil. He spoke briefly, aphoristically.

"The mouldboard plough is the worst enemy of steppeland farming. I think it's worth trying my system in your area, although perhaps you've got something smarter, something newer in mind?"

"What you want to do is to reduce the amount of tillage to the minimum! Turn up the virgin soil, but then touch it as little as possible."

"Fallow—that's the main factor in steppeland cropping. You won't get grain if your virgin lands don't have fallow."

"Weeds taking hold? That was to be expected. In some places they're already getting wheat mixed with wild oats. Later they'll be getting wild oats with some wheat in it. Some people get very upset. Wild oats, they say, are so tough, what's to do about them? But this weed, you know, is a feeble thing. It's only tough when there's a bad farmer around. Yes, it's good that you're sowing later. You have to wait and lure the wild oats on, then destroy them. After that you can sow. It takes strong nerves. Field cropping is no job for weaklings."

I was much enlightened. But why, in that case, the reader will ask, did this useful know-how not quickly spread across the virgin lands? My answer is that the soil has a worse enemy than the plough and the weed, and this enemy is all kinds of imposed "recommendations". There have been too many of them and they have cost the country too much for us not to realise that for agriculture, because of its very nature, commands from above are counter-productive. And although I must admit that I was sometimes very eager to "accelerate" and "step up" things, I restrained myself. People had to be given the chance to sort matters out for themselves, so that the know-how would evolve organically.

Naturally I asked the journalists to publicise the achievements of the best state farms. I also organised seminars and held conferences at the Central Committee. We gave high priority to developing a network of scientific institutions, getting them to study Soviet and world practice and find reliable ways of fighting soil erosion. I must mention the great work done by a team of scientists led by A. I. Baraev, now a Lenin Prize winner. I remember how insistently he pushed the importance of "small-scale irrigation" — letting the land lie fallow. And it was no accident that it was in the virgin lands of Kazakhstan that a soil-protective system of crop farming was subsequently devised.

We did all we could to defend the fallow and I have an interesting document to cite in this connection. A conference of specialists was being held in my office. It was 9 June, 1955, at the very peak of the drought. The heat was terrible, the fields were burning, and we had to talk about the future — about the plan for the development of Kazakhstan's agriculture over the whole five-year period. Here is part of the minutes of that meeting which shows how the question was treated at that time:

Comrade Melnik (the republic's Minister of Agriculture): Now about crop rotation. In view of the introduction of millions of hectares of virgin lands to cultivation we shall have to allocate a large amount of arable land to fallow. We have to sow wheat on wheat for three years, but in the fourth year we have to let it lie fallow. If we allocate only one-and-a-half million hectares a year to fallow, as has been suggested, by 1960 we will have had fallow on not more than one-sixth of all arable land. From the soil technology point of view this is very bad. Even if we find another two million hectares of virgin land by 1960 to expand the amount of arable land, in our current estimates for 1960 we will still have to somewhat reduce the amount of arable land allotted to grain. This is the only way we can ensure proper farming practices. And this must be done at all costs. Otherwise we will ruin the soil in the first rotation.

Comrade Brezhnev: Does anyone disagree?

Comrade Melnik: The decision of the Kazakh Central Committee and the republic's Council of Ministers, which stipulates a different figure for grain sowings, disagrees. The point is to change this previous decision, because when it was calculated there was a great deal that we could not yet accurately allow for.

Comrade Brezhnev: We have to get things straight on the subject of fallow. It seems we have reached something of a deadlock. Is this connected with our decision?

Comrade Melnik: Yes, we are tied by it.

Comrade Brezhnev: We must work on the basis of economic efficiency. We need a serious and sober estimate dictated by economic conditions. It already looks as if we must move into lower-moisture, poorer-quality land. I think we can accept that we will be able to find another couple of million hectares. But how about the total yield? Aren't you taking too much for fallow?

Comrade Melnik: No, we are not. Everything has been considered and agreed upon with the regions.

Comrade Arystanbekov (Deputy Minister of State Farms for the republic). We must bring the area of fallow up to between 16 and 18 per cent. Only then will we be able to reach the targets that have been set.

Comrade Brezhnev: But how does it work out? If on average for the republic we have, say, 17 per cent fallow, will we get the required total yield? Remember that with regard to total yield

Kazakhstan is in a very special position. The Party and the government will be keeping a strict eye on us. We can't chop and change.
We must have fallow, but how much? How much was there before
we started in the virgin lands?

Comrade Andrianova (head of the Scientific Board of the
republic's Ministry of Agriculture): In 1940 there was 18 per cent.
For our zone, fallow is the foundation of crop farming. In addition,
I want to mention perennial grass. I have in mind the zones
threatened by wind erosion. In those zones we must adopt a longer
crop rotation that includes grass as an anchor for the soil. This factor is not taken into account in the estimates. Besides the Maltsev
crop rotation there must be rotations that include perennial grasses.

Comrade Brezhnev: The idea is all right. . . . But what kind of
lucerne will the Pavlodar people, for instance, have this year?
They'll have neither grass nor anchorage.

Comrade Andrianova: They are not doing anything about grass
there at the moment, but they'll have to sometime. Otherwise the
erosion in that region will be worse than it's ever been anywhere.
Wind erosion will become a terrible scourge for us if we don't start
protecting ourselves against it now. This should be reflected in our
plans and estimates for the five-year period.

Comrade Brezhnev: I agree with you. It is clear that our
memorandum to the CPSU Central Committee and the government
should state plainly that grain production in the republic will reach
a certain level and stop there. This is quite understandable. In two
years we will open up 18 million hectares and we will sow wheat on
wheat for three years in succession, but it can't go on like that. The
target we tentatively set earlier was an arbitrary figure, it was what
we wanted to achieve. Later on we will be able to reach the target by
adding large areas of virgin land, not by rapacious use of the soil.

Comrade Melnik: There isn't much time for drawing up the
memorandum, only two or three days.

Comrade Brezhnev: Let the Central Committee secretary Fazyl
Karibzhanovich Karibzhanov take charge of that. He will get you all

together in his office and you can write it page by page day and night.

Comrade Melnik: That will mean closing down the ministry.

Comrade Brezhnev: This work is more important than anything else. Make the memorandum short and readable. Only figures and conclusions. Don't complicate it, don't try to be subtle. Everything must be clear and precise.

The memorandum was drawn up and sent to Moscow. Time has shown that our estimates were correct.

In February 1956, at the 20th Party Congress, I was proud to be able to report that the virgin lands project was a success. In two years the republic's sowing area had been expanded to 27 million hectares. There were 23 million under grain, and of these eighteen were under wheat—four times as much as before the project was launched. On behalf of all the virgin landers I assured the congress that Kazakhstan could produce sixteen million or more tonnes of grain per year.

But I did not consider that everything had been done and completed, that all our difficulties were over, so I stated further:

"The Kazakhstan Party organisation takes into account the fact that now when the republic's sowing area is being brought up to 27 million hectares, our main potential for further increases in grain production lies in raising yields. In this sphere we still have many shortcomings. In connection with the opening up of the virgin lands it has become an urgent matter to work out a system of farm management which takes into account the local peculiarities of each collective or state farm in order to ensure the best use of the land and preserve soil fertility. This is a big proposition. We request the Academy of Sciences, the Soviet Academy of Agricultural Sciences, and the Central Ministries of Agriculture and State Farms to help us so that the great work of developing the virgin lands can be brought to a successful conclusion."

In 1956 the great moment came for the virgin lands. A huge harvest was grown on the Kazakhstan steppe and instead of the promised ten million tonnes the republic supplied the state with *sixteen million* tonnes. I was truly happy when in that year Kazakhstan was awarded its first Order of Lenin for the sixteen million tonnes of virgin land grain. For it was that first monster harvest that first ensured the status of the virgin lands, a status that was never shaken either by the ravages of the elements or by the voluntarist decisions that intensified their effect.

Unfortunately, I was not able to see that gigantic harvest that had absorbed so much energy and effort. At the 20th Congress I was again elected secretary of the CPSU Central Committee.

That evening Kunaev, Satpaev, Zhurin, Makarin and other Kazakhstan colleagues came to congratulate me at the Moskva Hotel, where I was staying at the time. It was a hurried, affectionate and somehow wistful parting. They were anxious to get home and I was thinking about my new job. But I do want to say that it was sad to bid goodbye to the friends, the steppe I had grown to love, and the people, the virgin landers, who were so near and dear to me.

*   *   *

Luckily, this parting proved to be not a very long one. The virgin lands, which had formed such a precious and important period in my life, continued to excite and attract me. And after an interval taken up with other work, I turned to the virgin lands again. One of my many duties as General Secretary of the CPSU Central Committee was to support the soil-protective system of crop farming in the virgin lands evolved by Soviet scientists under A. I. Baraev. This system has now been introduced and has protected the virgin lands from wind erosion. We were able to apply it in a very short space of time over a huge area, including other steppeland zones of the country, and thus reinforced the recommendations of science with the power of technology.

Even today I take a constant interest in the virgin lands and often visit Kazakhstan. And I can say that I see there the realisation of my dream and the dream of hundreds of thousands of virgin landers.

Of course, by no means everything has been accomplished in the

virgin steppe. The potential there is still enormous. But that is a different subject. I want to speak of what has been achieved already, of
things that are both heartening and impressive.

The virgin lands project in Kazakhstan was not only on an enormous scale, but also economically profitable. I will cite figures to
prove this. In the past 24 years Kazakhstan has sold the state more
than 250 million tonnes of grain. In the same period, from 1954 to
1977 inclusive, total expenditure on the republic's agriculture — I
stress, all its agriculture, not just the virgin lands — amounted to
21.1 billion rubles. And the turnover tax from the sale of grain in
these years has yielded 27.2 billion rubles, that is to say, the country
has made a clear profit of 6.1 billion rubles. Moreover, one must
bear in mind that the fixed and working assets of the Kazakhstan
collective and state farms today amount to 15 billion rubles. So all
the work and all the expenditure have been recouped and have
returned a profit in the minimum amount of time. That is the splendid result of the most impressive battle for grain in the history of
mankind! The ancient steppe proved to be a giant. Transformed by
human labour, it has brought stability to our whole agriculture and
guaranteed a steady and adequate supply of grain. And the soil is
still building up its potential.

Fly across the vast expanses of the steppe. You will see not only
cornfields, but also the ribbons of metalled road, settlements,
railways, power lines, elevators, industrial complexes, factories and
cities. It was the mighty grain of the former feather-grass lands that
brought all this to life.

I remember, for example, what Akmolinsk was like when I first
saw it. Low clay-walled houses, narrow streets, a mere 80,000 inhabitants. . . . But today? The city, now called Tselinograd (Virgin
Land Town), has three times as many people. It has been almost entirely rebuilt, redesigned. It has dozens of industrial enterprises,
four institutes of higher education and fifteen technical colleges,
which in the past three years alone have trained more than 20,000
specialists.

The virgin lands provided a mighty push for the development of Kazakhstan's productive forces, its economy, science and culture. Major industrial complexes have come into being, ninety new cities have sprung up, including such famous places as Rudny, Ekibastuz, Yermak, Kentau, Arkalyk and Shevchenko. The republic is a producer of coal and oil, iron and steel, non-ferrous metals, mineral fertilizers, modern machine tools, machines and tractors. And no one is surprised that in once backward Kazakhstan a fast-breeder reactor has been put into operation.

Kazakhstan's star shines ever brighter in the constellation of the fraternal republics. Its development is measured in years and five-year plans, but it was all discussed, conceived, mulled over long ago. Many features of the face that this land presents to the world today were charted nearly a quarter of a century ago, when my office at the Central Committee became more and more often a meeting place for scientists, prospectors, planning experts and designers. It demanded much attention, time and effort.

Need I say how happy I am now with what I see: a gigantic agro-industrial complex has taken shape in the area. It exerts a powerful influence on the economy of the whole country. And the epic of the virgin lands has once again shown the world the fine moral qualities of Soviet people. It has become a symbol of selfless service to the homeland, a great achievement of the socialist era.